"Captivating . . . In many ways, Ross is a modern-day Benjamin of Tudela, the tenth-century Spanish Jewish traveler who chronicled his discovery of Jews in the diaspora. However, unlike his predecessor, Ross visits groups with atypical Jewish origins. . . . Ross provides an exciting, in-depth look at [these] unusual communities and sheds new light on the age-old question, Who is a Jew? This excellent book is well worth reading."

—*Hadassah Magazine*

"[Ross] describes these communities sympathetically and with detail, while the reader is left in awe at the tens of thousands who still yearn for Israel."

—*The Jerusalem Post*

"This useful travelogue, mingled with history, adds to our knowledge of unusual Jewish communities in different parts of the world."

—*American Jewish World*

"The reader meets real individuals here, not just groups."

—*San Jose Mercury News*

FRAGILE BRANCHES

Travels Through the Jewish Diaspora

JAMES R. ROSS

RIVERHEAD BOOKS

NEW YORK

RIVERHEAD BOOKS
Published by The Berkley Publishing Group
A division of Penguin Putnam Inc.
375 Hudson Street
New York, New York 10014

Unless indicated otherwise, the material in this book comes from my
interviews with the principal subjects, and from firsthand observation.
All newspaper and magazine articles were retrieved from Lexis-Nexis
Academic Universe. Translations from the Bible are from *The
Holy Scriptures* (Jewish Publication Society, 1961) and *The Tanakh: The New
JPS Translation According to the Traditional Hebrew Text* (Jewish Publication
Society, 1985), copyright © 1985 by the Jewish Publication Society, used by
permission. Translations of Hebrew prayers are from *Gates of Prayer* (New
York: Central Conference of American Rabbis, 1977).

Published simultaneously in Canada.

First Riverhead hardcover edition: September 2000
First Riverhead trade paperback edition: September 2001
Riverhead trade paperback ISBN: 1-57322-895-8

Visit our website at
www.penguinputnam.com

The Library of Congress has catalogued the Riverhead hardcover edition as follows:

Ross, James R.
      Fragile branches: travels through the Jewish diaspora /
      James R. Ross.
          p.   cm.
      Includes bibliographical references.
      ISBN 1-57322-165-1
      1. Jews—Civilization.   2. Jewish diaspora.
      3. Ross, James R.—Journeys.   I. Title.
DS134 .R65   2000   00-040291
909'.04924—dc21

Printed in the United States of America

10   9   8   7   6   5   4   3   2   1

The Laramie County
Community College
Ludden Library

would like to thank

*Mark
Elliott*

for donating this book
to our collection

Contents

Fragile Branches

INTRODUCTION

I met Paulo Sicsu inside the gates of a small Jewish cemetery in Parintins, a dusty island town between the banks of the Amazon river. Paulo, a young man with a dark, close-cropped beard and doleful blue eyes, was looking down at a weathered gravestone inscribed with a Jewish star and the name of his great-grandfather Abraham Joseph Sicsu. There were sixty-six other stones in the cemetery, nearly all of them bearing Moroccan Jewish names, from as early as 1886.

Paulo spoke in a hushed voice, as if he were afraid of disturbing the dead. Jacques Cukierkorn, a Brazilian-born rabbi, translated for me from the Portuguese. Paulo said he lived here in Parintins and worked as a photographer, gesturing at the camera bag that hung over his shoulder. His great-grandfather, from a religious Moroccan Sephardic family, had come from Tangier as a teenager more than a hundred years before, hoping to make his fortune in the rubber trade.

Abraham had worshiped with a small group of Jewish men on the Sabbath but abandoned most of his Jewish traditions. He lived with a local girl, barely in her teens, and they raised five children, including Paulo's grandfather, as Protestants. By the time Paulo's father was a young man, the family had completely lost touch with Judaism. Paulo still yearned for some connection to his past.

"I keep coming here, seeking my traditions," Paulo said, "but there's no one to tell me what to do."

I asked Rabbi Cukierkorn if he would recite the mourner's *kaddish,* the ancient Aramaic prayer through which Judaism commemorates the dead by celebrating God and life, over Abraham's grave. The rabbi prayed as Paulo wept quietly.

"I have another favor to ask," I said when the rabbi had finished. "I'd like you to write out a transliteration of the *kaddish* for him."

"I can't do that," Rabbi Cukierkorn said. "He's not Jewish."

"I thought you were a Reform rabbi," I said, teasing him a bit. "I didn't know you were so strict."

The rabbi reluctantly scribbled the transliterated prayer on one of my notebook pages and handed it to Paulo, whose still-tearful eyes conveyed his thanks.

IN ISOLATED TOWNS and villages throughout the world, from the Amazon rain forest to the hills of northeastern

India, I found people and communities that are discovering connections to Judaism and inventing new forms of Jewish life. Some are former Christians or Muslims who have been inspired by charismatic leaders to follow practices recorded in the Hebrew Bible; others believe their ancestors were Jews and have proclaimed that they are returning to traditions lost through years of persecution or assimilation. All of them desperately want to be accepted and recognized as Jews.

Like most religions, Judaism has continually reinvented itself. The Hebrews first emerged from a polyglot of tribes and conquered peoples. Descent was based on paternity; many Hebrew forefathers, from Abraham to Moses, intermarried with women from other tribes. As the Hebrew people became a nation, a countless number of converts joined them. Many came from conquered tribes who were forced to convert.

In subsequent generations, after the nation suffered invasions and defeats, Jews were deported or migrated to other lands. They eventually dispersed to nearly every nation. Jewish rituals, languages, customs, and values—even Jewish law and Jewish history—were perpetually reshaped under the influences of these diverse cultures.

Scholars believe that the Jews of Persia and Mesopotamia borrowed ideas about resurrection from the Zoroastrians and later brought them to ancient Israel. Under Greek influence in the second century B.C.E., Jews in the diaspora reinterpreted the Bible both literally and allegorically, linking the stories and characters to moral lessons and philosophical principles. They also learned the rabbinic method of argument and analysis from the Greeks.

The emergence of new Jewish sects—groups that separated from the predominant forms of Judaism yet remained Jews—has contributed to the ongoing reinvention of Judaism throughout the ages as well. Each group has left its mark and changed the contours of Judaism. One of the first major sects was the Samaritans, who built a temple on Mt. Gerizim, near modern-day Nablus, in the fourth century B.C.E. After their temple was destroyed two centuries later, Samaritans began to disperse throughout northern Africa, southern Europe, and the Middle East. At one time, they had hundreds of thousands of followers. They maintained that they were the true descendants of the Hebrew people of the Bible. Jewish authorities had always questioned that claim—they believed that the Samaritans descended from foreigners who converted after the Assyrians deported them to Israel—yet accepted the Samaritans as Jews. By the end of the third century C.E., however, when the Samaritans had developed their own liturgy, schools, and synagogues, the rabbis ruled that the Samaritans were heretics, not Jews. Today there are about six hundred surviving Samaritans, half of them living in Holon, near Tel Aviv, and half in a village near Nablus in the West Bank. Rabbis now consider the Samaritans who live in Israel to be Jews; those who live in the West Bank can receive Israeli citizenship for "human and economic reasons."

From the second century B.C.E. until the destruction of the Second Temple in 70 C.E., other new sects competed to become the ruling religious authority. The Essenes questioned the importance of the Temple and priests and developed their own purification rites. Some of them withdrew to form ascetic communities. The Sadducee sect was made up of high priests and aristocrats who adapted to Greek culture while at the same time emphasized the importance of the Temple and sacrifices. The Pharisee sect, which, unlike the Sadducees, was made up of both priests and common people, opposed the Sadducees and stressed the importance of prayer, laws of purity, and oral law. The rabbinic movement, which developed after the Roman conquest, inherited many Pharisee beliefs and practices. Even Christianity first materialized as a new form of Judaism, reinterpreting some traditions, such as Passover, and developing new ones.

In the eighth century C.E., a new sect known as the Karaites challenged the rabbis in the same way the Sadducees had challenged the Pharisees. They rejected the authority of the rabbis and the oral law, which had been codified in the Talmud. The Karaites proclaimed that every Jew who reads the Torah closely can find the plain meaning of the text on his own. Many of their practices were based on the way Jews worshiped in the ancient Temples in Jerusalem. Karaites survive today as one of the few remaining sects of Judaism, a separate group that is still considered Jewish (see chapter 6).

In the seventeenth century C.E., another mass movement emerged that undermined the rabbinic authorities. Sabbatai Zevi, a Jewish rabbinic student and mystic, claimed that he heard voices urging him to reject many sacred beliefs and eventually telling him that he was the Messiah. The rabbis excommunicated him, yet he gathered nearly a million followers before the Turkish sultan forced him to renounce his Judaism and convert to Islam. His following survives today in Turkey, where hundreds of so-called Donmeh secretly carry out Sabbatean

practices; a small number hope to be accepted as Jews and settle in Israel.

Zevi and others who later claimed to be the Messiah un-
derscored the failure of the rabbis, according to some historians,
to appeal to the poor and the uneducated. That failure spawned
another sect, Hasidism, which soon dominated Eastern European Judaism. The Hasids embraced mysticism and spirituality
rather than scholarship, and drew millions of followers by the
middle of the nineteenth century. Instead of confronting this
fragmented rebellion, rabbinic authorities absorbed it by adopt-
ing many Hasidic beliefs and practices. Today's ultra-Orthodox
Jews are the inheritors of this melding of the mystical and the
scholarly.

The idea of a Jewish orthodoxy didn't formally emerge until
the nineteenth century. It developed in response to Reform Judaism, a movement founded in Germany which inspired Jews to
take active roles outside the ghetto and in the surrounding
community. The success of Reform Jews and resentment against
them in German society, fueled the Nazis' virulent anti-
Semitism; some ultra-Orthodox Jews have suggested that the
Holocaust was God's punishment for Jewish assimilation.

The diaspora has spawned many Jewish customs and languages. Kurdistani Jews celebrate Shavuot, the Festival of
Weeks, by staging mock battles in the mountains close to where
Noah's ark may have landed. "Mountain Jews" in the Cauca-
sus recite many of their prayers in the Jewish dialect of Tat, a
nearly lost western Iranian language. Some descendants of Spanish Jews still speak Ladino, a mixture of Spanish, Hebrew, Arabic, and several other tongues. American Jews, adapting to

their Christian surroundings, have inflated the importance of Hanukkah, a minor Jewish holiday, which usually takes place close to Christmas. Jewish foods, from couscous to latkes, also borrow from a wide range of cultures.

Reform and Conservative Judaism now have become the dominant forms of Jewish life in the United States. These new forms, along with widespread intermarriage and greater acceptance of converts, have again shifted the boundaries of Judaism. American Jewry has become a mix of ancient and modern values, traditions, and cultures.

The same reinvention is underway in Israel, where secular Jews predominate and Reform and Conservative Jewry are gaining followers, though Orthodox Jews retain the voice of Jewish legal authority. In Israel, only Orthodox rabbis can perform legal marriages, divorces, and conversions. Israeli law gives the rabbinic courts the right to decide who should be considered a Jew. Like members of dozens of other sects and movements throughout Jewish history, the Orthodox rabbis have fought any changes that would diminish their authority.

The Orthodox rabbis in Israel generally recognize as Jews only those who can prove a continuous maternal lineage or those who have been converted by fellow Orthodox rabbis. Nonetheless, defining who is a Jew is more a political than a theological question, as it has been throughout Jewish history. A 1970 amendment expanded Israel's Law of Return to permit immigration of those with one parent or grandparent who was a Jew, as well as non-Jewish spouses. Hundreds of thousands of immigrants from the former Soviet Union, many with only marginal connections to Judaism, settled in Israel under this amendment and were eligible for government assistance. In the late 1980s, Israeli authorities succumbed to international humanitarian appeals and agreed to allow Ethiopia's Beta Israel, suffering during civil war and famine, to settle in Israel. The rabbis drew on the journals of a mysterious ninth-century traveler to support the Ethiopians' questionable claim that they were descendants of the mythic Ten Lost Tribes dispersed from ancient Israel after the Assyrian conquest more than 2,700 years ago. Most scholars believe the Beta Israel descended from converts who had learned about the Hebrew people from Christian missionaries in the fourteenth and fifteenth centuries.

In recent years, as Israel has become wealthier and the drive to settle the occupied territories has slowed, its leaders have been reluctant to accept new immigrants, despite the Law of Return. Indians, Peruvians, and black Africans who practice Judaism face bureaucratic barriers and long delays from political and religious officials. Many Israelis fear large influxes of poor people from the Third World; rabbis have challenged their origins and their moti ions.

Among the communities I visited, however, I found people who had sacrificed their jobs, friends, and even their families in their struggle to become Jews. Undoubtedly, some of them are driven, at least in part, by economic opportunities that might await them in Israel. Yet I was convinced that nearly everyone I met was sincere in his or her commitment to Judaism.

WHAT COULD MOTIVATE people to declare themselves Jews in places that seem so hostile and foreign to Jewish life? Why would Africans, Asians, and Latin Americans identify with a religion that often seems to reject outsiders?

Part of the answer lies in the enduring appeal of the Hebrew Bible, the text that has guided Jews for millennia. Its vivid characters and compelling stories—from God's rescue of Isaac, as his father prepared to sacrifice him, to Moses' smashing of the golden calf after he received God's commandments on Mt. Sinai—are crafted in spare, evocative language. Yet the power of the Hebrew Bible is far greater than its captivating narratives or poetic phrasing. It appeals on a universal level as the story of mankind's struggle to find its place in the world.

These isolated communities are drawn to Judaism also because of the Bible's declaration that the Jews are the "chosen people." This special status in the eyes of God can have resonance for anyone who seeks a better life and feels constrained by a dominant religion and culture. Jews almost always have lived as a minority culture, sustaining their unique identity while adapting to their surroundings. They have survived massacres, expulsions, torture, pogroms, and near extinction. Oppressed peoples everywhere—minorities, the poor, those who simply don't fit in—often are able to identify with the Jewish people.

Despite the often bleak history of the Jews, many see Judaism as a religion of hope. Jewish prayers are filled with messages of hope and redemption, even for those who have transgressed. There is hope as well in biblical proclamations that Jews will serve as a "light unto the nations" and help summon an age of peace.

THE SEARCH FOR my own Jewish identity also is part of these stories. My father's father was an Orthodox Jew from Eastern Europe who was sent to *yeshiva* at age four to be trained as a rabbi. Between classes, however, he read forbidden Russian novels and learned about faraway places. At age fourteen, he left the *yeshiva*, returned to his small village, and announced his plans to leave for America, the golden land, where some of his relatives had settled. He taught Hebrew for a year to pay for tickets so both he and his father could sail across the Atlantic in steerage on an ocean liner. He joined his relatives in southern Maine—the first villagers to arrive had intended to settle in Portland, Oregon, but were directed to Portland, Maine, instead—and sold clothes and dry goods door-to-door. When he had earned enough to start a family, he married a cousin who also had come from his village.

My grandfather remained religious but accommodating. After he opened his own dry-goods store, he worked on Saturdays, confident that God wouldn't deny him a chance to make a living. Yet he never turned on lights or operated his cash register on the Sabbath—he could do all the figures in his head. All four of his children went to college, and the oldest, my father, graduated from Yale Medical School and became a pediatrician.

My mother's family also came to the United States from Europe, but like many immigrants of the late nineteenth and early twentieth centuries, they said little about their past and tried to assimilate into American culture. They lived in Boston, where they joined a Reform synagogue whose rabbis at one time advocated intermarriage and held services on Sundays. My parents met when my father was in medical school, and they were married at the Reform synagogue in Boston. To please my grandfather, the rabbi honored my father's request to wear a skullcap at the wedding. After serving as a medical officer in the Pacific, my father returned to southern Maine to practice.

There were only a handful of Jewish families in the small town where I grew up, but my parents kept a kosher home, attended services with my sister and me every Friday night, and sent me to Hebrew school and Jewish summer camps. Like many young American Jews, I lost touch with my religion when I left home for college. I rarely attended services, and paid little attention to Judaism.

I began to rediscover my Judaism in the late 1980s, nearly ten thousand miles from home. After two summers of teaching journalism in Shanghai, China, I read a brief account of the 20,000 European Jewish refugees who had escaped the Nazis and spent the war years in Shanghai. I decided to write a book about their community, not realizing that this would bring me back to my roots.

For more than two years I traveled to China, Australia, Israel, Germany, Austria, and throughout the United States, interviewing survivors from that refugee community. They welcomed me into their homes, told me their stories, and reawakened me to the joy of being a member of the Jewish people. In 1994, I completed *Escape to Shanghai: A Jewish Community in China.* It was too late to share the book with my father, who had died in 1988, but Judaism became a part of my home and I began to integrate my newfound enthusiasm for my religion with my career as a journalist and writer.

Judaism has all but disappeared in China; I continued my search for unusual stories elsewhere in the diaspora. I spent three weeks with members of the Jewish community in Buenos Aires shortly after the July 1994 bombing of a Jewish center there. I interviewed survivors of the attack, attended High Holiday services, and marveled at the rich cultural and intellectual life of Argentine Jews. They have maintained a Jewish identity even though few of them follow Jewish religious practices. I decided to look for other varieties of Jewish life in foreign lands.

On my return from South America, I learned about a group called Kulanu (Hebrew for "all of us") and their visit to the self-proclaimed Jews in Uganda. They led me to Rabbi Cukierkorn, a Brazilian-born Reform rabbi who had studied the secret Jews in Brazil and was then leading a congregation in Sharon, Pennsylvania. I visited him for a weekend to discuss my research and to speak to his congregation about the Shanghai Jews. A few months later, we went together to search for secret Jews in Brazil and Moroccan Jews in the Amazon. In the months that followed, I traveled to Uganda, Peru, India, and Israel to interview members of other remote communities.

The stories I discovered made me proud to be part of such a diverse and enduring people. They also made me question my assumptions about what it means to be a Jew. Most of these communities, cut off from any contact with living Jews, learned their practices by reading about the Hebrews of the Bible. They integrated these practices with the origins and customs of their surrounding communities—as Jews have done since they first were exiled from ancient Israel. But are they Jews? Do these groups in Asia, Africa, and Latin America have as much right to call themselves Jews as Sadducees, Sabbateans, and Essenes once did and as Reform, Conservative, and secular Jews do today?

The diversity of the Jewish people, along with their history of dispersion, intermarriage, and conversion, make it nearly impossible to define who is a Jew. Perhaps a more meaningful question is: "Who decides who is a Jew?" Should a handful of ultra-Orthodox authorities in Israel have the right to judge what they identify as "Torah-true" Judaism? Or should Jews welcome the diversity that has been central to Jewish life throughout its history? These disparate communities are searching for their places in the world. How we, both Jews and non-Jews, respond to them is nothing less than a reflection of how we look at ourselves.

. . . borrowed ideas about resurrection from the Zoroastrians . . . Shaul Shaked, "Iranian Influence on Judaism: First Century B.C.E. to Second Century C.E.," in *The Cambridge History of Judaism,* vol 1, W. D. Davies and Louis Finkelstein, eds. (New York: Cambridge University Press, 1984), p. 323.

Under Greek influence . . . Shaye J. D. Cohen, *From the Maccabees to the Mishnah* (Philadelphia: The Westminster Press, 1987), p. 207.

. . . rabbis ruled that the Samaritans were heretics, not Jews Alan D. Crown, "Redating the Schism Between the Judaeans and the Samaritans," *Jewish Quarterly Review* 82, nos. 1–2 (July–October 1991): 17–50.

. . . "human and economic reasons." Evelyn Gordon, "Samaritans

Petition Court to Restore Immigrant Status," *Jerusalem Post*, August 2, 1993; "Samaritans Caught Between Israel and Palestinians," *Reuters North American Wire*, August 25, 1997; Haim Shapiro, "A Challenge for the Samaritans," *Jerusalem Post*, September 26, 1999.

From the second century B.C.E. . . . . Christianity first materialized as a new form of Judaism . . .   Cohen, *From the Maccabees to the Mishnah*, pp. 143–71.

In the seventeenth century C.E. . . . and convert to Islam.   Max I. Dimont, *Jews, God and History* (New York: Penguin, 1994), pp. 282–84.

. . . melding of the mystical and scholarly.   Ibid., pp. 286–88.

The idea of Jewish orthodoxy . . .   Cohen, *From the Maccabees to the Mishnah*, p. 134.

Kurdistani Jews celebrate Shavuot . . .   Yona Sabar, *The Folk Literature of the Kurdistani Jews: An Anthology* (New Haven: Yale University Press, 1982), p. xxvi.

The rabbis drew on the journals . . .   Rabbi Eliyahu Avichail, *The Tribes of Israel* (Jerusalem: Amishav, 1989), p. 46.

Chapter One

THE ABAYUDAYA

The sun has set behind the vast, rolling foothills of Uganda's Mt. Elgon, and I am enveloped in darkness. In the clear air on Nabugoye Hill, with no lights visible for miles, I can see thousands of stars. Even Orion's sword shines brightly. I walk slowly up the dirt path, following the sounds of a congregation singing a familiar hymn. It is *Lecha Dodi,* the sixteenth-century prayer sung on Friday nights by Jews on every continent:

> Come, my beloved, to meet the bride;
> Let us welcome the presence of the Sabbath.

The words are in Hebrew, but the tune is unusual, a rising and falling rhythm that follows a jazzlike beat. I step up into a one-story brick building—there is no door—and can begin to distinguish the dark faces in the flickering light of the Sabbath candles. Then I walk across the floor to join the men and boys who stand near a wooden bench that lines one wall. A young man with a broad-brimmed black hat and tortoiseshell glasses welcomes me with the customary Sabbath greeting, *"Shabbat Shalom,"* and hands me a Hebrew and English prayer book, opened to the end of the Friday-night psalms. The dozen men around me wear simple dark trousers, white shirts, and knitted orange, purple, and green skullcaps that cover the tops and sides of their heads, like Muslim prayer caps, embroidered with *menorahs* and Stars of David. A few of the older men are barefoot. Directly opposite us, standing near the other wall, ten women in loose, brightly colored dresses hold infants in their arms as they sway to the melody and sing in harmony.

Between us on a long table are the Sabbath candles, an oil lamp, a metal decanter surrounded by wine cups, and a braided loaf of *challah* wrapped in a white cloth, smelling fresh and sweet. On a raised platform in the center of the synagogue, a tall and very thin young man wearing a long white robe and a white cap leads the prayers from behind a lectern, which is covered with a gold, purple, and scarlet cloth. He faces a simple white curtain decorated with a Star of David on the other side of the table. Behind the curtain is a Torah, the sacred parchment scroll containing the meticulously hand-lettered Hebrew words of the Five Books of Moses, the source of a tradition that has uplifted and unified Jews throughout the world for 4,000 years.

Here in Uganda, the heart of East Africa, this group of

worshipers who call themselves Abayudaya have recently begun to observe this tradition. Founded by a great warrior and statesman in 1919, the Abayudaya—the word for Jew in their native Luganda—initially practiced an odd mix of customs and rituals. Over the years, based on their contacts with visiting Jews, they have come to adopt more Orthodox Jewish practices. Many in the community follow Jewish laws for sexual purity, circumcision, and slaughtering animals; they observe the Sabbath and holidays with prayers and rituals shared by Jews everywhere. Yet outside of Uganda they are not considered Jews.

Gershom Sizomu, the young man in the broad-brimmed hat, serves as one of the community's religious leaders and teachers, as well as its ritual slaughterer. He has written Orthodox rabbis in England and Israel asking them to send a Jewish court—a group of three rabbis who approve candidates for conversion—but they have not replied. "The important recognition comes from God, not individuals," Gershom says as we walk to the entrance of the synagogue after services. "Even when Orthodox Jews say we are not Jews, we feel we are Jews in the eyes of God."

Conversion would give the Abayudaya the right to live in Israel, which would provide some protection from an uncertain future in Uganda's still-fragile democracy.

In their brief history, the Abayudaya have endured persecution, poverty, isolation, near dissolution, dictatorship, civil war, famine, and threats of arrest and imprisonment. "I feel Israel may be the safest place for us," Gershom says. "Conversion is more of a political issue than a religious one."

SEMEI KAKUNGULU WAS a mythic figure, tall, powerful, and somber, with the bearing of a prince and the visage of a prophet. According to biographer Michael Twaddle, his military and political skills helped propel Uganda into the modern era, yet his origins, and much about his life, remain elusive. As Kakungulu's religious and tribal loyalties changed, he and his followers altered facts about his life, including his birthplace and parentage. Even after Kakungulu's death, his descendants continued to manipulate his biography. Twaddle concludes that Kakungulu was born about 1868, probably in the Koki kingdom near the western shore of Lake Victoria. He was the son or adopted son of an official of the Koki court and served the king as a skilled elephant hunter. Rivalries in the court apparently forced him to leave, at about age sixteen, for the kingdom of Buganda, on the north shore of Lake Victoria. It was there that he achieved his reputation as a fearless warrior who smoked hemp, let his hair grow long and wild, and plundered other tribes on behalf of the Buganda king.

Islam, introduced by Arab traders in the middle of the nineteenth century, was initially the dominant nontribal religion in the kingdom. Anglican missionaries were permitted to settle near the court in the late 1870s. Young pages like Kakungulu saw the missionaries from England as possible allies in their palace power struggles. At night, between hunting trips, Kakungulu secretly learned to read Swahili and studied the Bible and Christianity with one of the missionaries, Alexander Mackay. Literacy gave Kakungulu status; and belief in God and in an afterlife appealed to a man who risked his life nearly every day. At first, it seems, Christianity didn't displace his tribal beliefs but merely supplemented them. Yet Kakungulu's later attraction to Judaism wasn't a radical departure from what Mackay had taught him. Evangelical Anglicans had appropriated much from ancient Judaism and considered themselves to be the chosen people.

At about the same time Kakungulu was being drawn to Christianity, other pages in the court adopted a stricter form of Islam, introduced by Sudanese fundamentalists. After the king massacred scores of the radical Muslims, they staged a coup. Years of warfare followed. Kakungulu initially lost his chieftancy, but his adeptness in switching loyalties and his bravery in battle helped him regain power. In the 1890s, British colonists recruited Kakungulu to lead his followers in the successful battle to take control of Uganda. The British rewarded him with a land grant, and he and his followers chose to settle in the central highlands, where bananas, the staple food for Ganda warriors, were plentiful. Kakungulu soon adapted to the role of government bureaucrat. He founded the town of Mbale, which later became the third largest city in Uganda, built roads and bridges, and planted trees and crops throughout the region. But the British reneged on their promise to award Kakungulu a royal title and eventually transferred him to another post in Jinja, at the source of the Nile river on Lake Victoria. His dispute with the British continued, and he resigned his post in 1913 to return to Mbale.

Kakungulu's anger at the British and his continuing search for spirituality drew him to the Malakites, a new religious sect in

Mbale named after its founder, Malaki Musajakawa, a former Protestant. Like many African religions of the time, it incorporated a wide range of Western and tribal beliefs. The Malakites mixed tribalism with their own interpretations of the Hebrew Bible and New Testament, some of which mirrored Judaism, Christianity, and Christian Science. In the Buganda region alone, the Malakites attracted nearly 100,000 followers within two or three years. They practiced baptism, refused to eat pork, rejected idol worship, and declared Saturday as their day of rest. Kakungulu helped them develop a calendar based on his reading of the Book of Exodus, and wrote a pamphlet of texts and hymns. The new religion permitted men to have more than one wife at a time, reacting against the moral strictures of British Protestant and Catholic missionaries.

The Malakites' most radical doctrine, and the source of their real friction with the British, was their fervent opposition to the use of medicines. They based this belief on a passage from Jeremiah ("In vain dost thou use many medicines; There is no cure for thee") as well as their skepticism about Western medical care, which seemed to kill as many people as it cured. Africans with sleeping sickness—an often fatal disease carried by the tsetse fly—were placed in camps and usually died there; victims of venereal disease often suffered relapses after they were treated; and many cattle died soon after they were vaccinated. To Africans who had abandoned witchcraft under the influence of Islamic fundamentalists and English missionaries, Western medicine seemed like another form of paganism. The Malakites refused to enter a hospital or let the British inoculate them against smallpox or their cattle against rinderpest and other diseases.

Kakungulu's spiritual restlessness soon drove him apart from the Malakites as well. In 1918 he objected to communion services, suggesting that the Bible called for people to break bread in their homes. The following year, he told Malaki that the Bible commanded that all males be circumcised on the eighth day of life, the covenant that Abraham had made with God. This was a dramatic break not only from the Malakites but also from Gandan tribal ritual, which shunned any type of bodily mutilation. Malaki told Kakungulu that circumcision was a practice only among Jews.

"If this is the case," Kakungulu is said to have replied, "then from this day on I am a Jew (Abayudaya)." Kakungulu and his sons were circumcised, as were his male relatives, and soon after, so were thousands of followers. He gave his children biblical names—Abraham Ndaula, Judah Maccabee, Nimrod, Israel, Jonah, and Miriam—and built a house on his land in the western foothills of Mt. Elgon. There he established a new sect, "the community of Jews (Abayudaya) who trust in the Lord."

BLACK AFRICANS, INCLUDING the Beta Israel of Ethiopia and the Lemba of South Africa, have asserted links to the Jewish people that date back thousands of years. The original Beta Israel, popularly known by the derogatory term *Falasha*, claim to descend from the Lost Tribe of Dan, which disappeared in the eighth century B.C.E. It seems more likely, how-

ever, that their ancestors were Ethiopian Christians who formed
a religious group based on the Hebrew Bible about 500 years
ago. Their numbers grew from conversions of native Ethiopians and perhaps Jewish refugees from Yemen. Most of them
now live in Israel, although thousands remain stranded in refugee
camps in Ethiopia. The Lemba in southern Africa, who practice circumcision and do not eat pork, also claim their origins
in Ancient Israel thousands of years ago. Anthropologists have
concluded that the Lemba appropriated these practices when
white missionaries taught them about the Hebrew Bible. Geneticists have found, however, that many Lemba men carry
DNA sequences that are nearly unique to *cohanim*, Jewish
priests believed to descend from Moses' brother, Aaron. The se-
quence is almost as common among the priestly clan of the
Lemba as it is among Ashkenazi Jews who are believed to be
cohanim.

The most familiar tie between Uganda and the Jews, an ill-
fated plan to establish a Jewish homeland in East Africa, pre-
ceded the origin of the Abayudaya. Theodor Herzl, the founder
of modern Zionism, entertained an offer from the British in
1903 to donate land in Uganda—in territory that is now part
of Kenya—as an alternative to present-day Israel. The proposal
created a rift among early Zionists, who were torn between the
immediate need for a Jewish refuge and the historic links to Israel. The offer was rejected shortly after Herzl's death in 1904.

KAKUNGULU'S NEW RELIGION was an evangelical
version of Judaism that borrowed from Christianity, Islam, and

African tribal customs. The original Abayudaya followed both the Hebrew Bible and New Testament, removed their shoes like Muslims before entering a house of prayer, and beat African drums to summon their followers to services. They welcomed and encouraged converts, as early Jews had done for centuries, immersing them in a ritual bath near Kakungulu's home that was fed by a freshwater spring. Kakungulu attracted adherents by supplying them with clothes, seeds, and cattle. He provided them with a bar of soap every Friday, and invited them to his house for dinner after sundown on Saturday. Many followers were tenants on his large estate, to whom he offered reduced rent and exemption from some work if they joined the Abayudaya. He adopted orphans, including Gershom's father, and trained some of them to be teachers to instruct the converts. Kakungulu rewarded the teachers with gifts of land and their own synagogues. Gershom's father served as the religious leader for a small synagogue, and his congregants supported his family for more than a generation.

In 1922, Kakungulu compiled a ninety-page book of prayers and rituals that served as a guidebook for his teachers. He used quotations from the Bible to urge his followers to keep the Sabbath and obey the other commandments. The following year, he began the construction of a small synagogue near his home. The great warrior, statesman, and founder of Mbale became a religious leader. Kakungulu led the services, which included readings from the Book of Psalms and other passages from the Bible, and delivered passionate sermons expounding on the principles of his new faith.

The Abayudaya were spread over Kakungulu's broad land

holdings. They eventually formed communities with their own leadership and somewhat different practices. One group worshiped in a tiny mud hut down the hill in Namanyoyi. There also were synagogues in Palissa, where Kakungulu first settled, and Namutumba, nearly thirty miles from Mbale.

Missionaries urged Kakungulu to return to Christianity. In 1921, he received a letter from an English priest, pleading with him to follow the teachings of Jesus. In his reply, Kakungulu defended his faith by quoting from an English translation of the Hebrew Bible, including a passage from Zechariah 8:23— "Thus saith the Lord of Hosts: 'In those days it shall come to pass, that ten men shall take hold, out of all the languages of the nations, shall even take hold of the skirt of him that is a Jew, saying: We will go with you, for we have heard that God is with you.' " To Kakungulu and his followers, this passage prophesied that they should become Jews, that their numbers would grow, and that they would be accepted by all of the Jewish people.

Kakungulu's new religion separated him even further from the British, and in 1923, when Kakungulu was about fifty-five years old, they asked him to retire from his official post in Mbale. They added to this insult by attempting to take over some of Kakungulu's land in an area that is now the site of Makerere University. Kakungulu went to Kampala to contest the action. It was in court in Kampala that Kakungulu, for the first time, met a Jewish man, a trader whose name was Yosefu or Joseph. Little is known about him. Some elders recall that he was about forty, dark-skinned, and bearded, and he may have come from Ethiopia or Israel. Apparently he was well versed in

Jewish law. Joseph gave Kakungulu a Hebrew Bible and agreed to visit Mbale to teach the community about Judaism.

When Joseph told the Abayudaya that other Jews did not follow the New Testament or believe in Christ, Kakungulu then ripped the pages of the New Testament from his Bible. Joseph also taught them Jewish blessings, prayers, and the Hebrew alphabet, and instructed them in how to slaughter a chicken to make it kosher.

What makes the Abayudaya unique, and most likely accounts for their continued survival, is their desire to learn from the outside world. From its earliest days, the Abayudaya religion has adapted. Today, Abayudaya like Gershom maintain their respect for Kakungulu's practices and beliefs but have reshaped their religion based on the teachings of visiting rabbis and other Jews. This agility is part of their tradition. Kakungulu's religious convictions evolved and shifted throughout his life. Even after he declared himself a Jew, his searching continued.

Following Joseph's visit, Kakungulu announced plans to found a Jewish school. At the time, nearly all the Abayudaya children attended primary schools run by Muslims or Christian missionaries, and Kakungulu was worried that pressure from their peers and teachers, along with daily religious lessons, would lead the children away from their new religion. Even his eldest son, Abraham Ndaula, had been attracted to Christianity after years of attending an Anglican school. The Jewish school would provide not only basic education in reading, writing, and math but also religious lessons in the Hebrew Bible, Hebrew, and Jewish rituals that Joseph had taught the community. Kakungulu also began to compile a new prayer book, eliminating Christian practices, but never finished it. He died in 1928, apparently from pneumonia, still refusing medical treatment.

Without Kakungulu's charisma and generosity, his religion floundered in the decades after his death and many of his followers converted to Christianity or again became Malakites. Several teachers Kakungulu had trained competed bitterly to take over leadership of the community, and their rivalry further depleted the community. Yet they sustained their hope that Zechariah's prophecy would come to pass.

In 1937, an Indian-born Jew named David Solomon, who had come to Mbale to work for the water company, discovered the Abayudaya when he heard the drums beating to call them to Passover services. Solomon remained in Mbale for nearly thirty years and visited them regularly. Although he was not well educated in Judaism, he gave them clothes, Hebrew calendars, and an elementary Hebrew textbook, from which one of the elders learned to read Hebrew. They used the calendars to set the dates for celebrating the Jewish holidays.

Solomon tried for years to bring outside aid to the Abayudaya as their spirit and numbers diminished through years of isolation. By 1961, with less than 300 members remaining in the community, the Abayudaya were forced to give up the Jewish school that Kakungulu's son Abraham Ndaula had built after his father's death. Ndaula had paid the teachers' salaries and maintained the school for more than thirty years, even after he had converted to Christianity. In 1961, however, he told the Abayudaya that he could not afford to continue his support. Ndaula leased the school buildings to the Anglican church.

Ndaula planned to give the church both the land on Nabu-goye Hill and the buildings. The Abayudaya elders, most of whom had studied under Kakungulu, adamantly opposed giving up the land and pleaded with Ndaula to honor his father's name. It was sacred ground, they argued, and losing it would mean the end of Kakungulu's dream. Ndaula relented, but the church did not lose its ambition to take over the land. With their foothold on Nabugoye Hill, the Christian missionaries redoubled their efforts to convert the remaining Abayudaya to Christianity.

The following year, David Solomon finally succeeded in bringing the Abayudaya to the attention of other Jews when he arranged for Arye Oded, the Israeli ambassador to Kenya, to meet them. Over the next five years, Oded visited the community several times and attended services led by Samson Mugombe, whom Kakungulu had trained as a young man to be a teacher. Oded later wrote about Mugombe's service, which began with members of the congregation holding their raised palms before them and singing a passage from Deuteronomy. Kakungulu had composed the melody; the words were the song Moses had spoken to the people of Israel just before his death:

> Give ear, ye heavens, and I will speak;
> And let the earth hear the words of my mouth.
> My doctrine shall drop as the rain,
> My speech shall distill as the dew;
> As the small rain upon the tender grass,
> And as the showers upon the herb.
> For I will proclaim the name of the Lord;
> Ascribe ye greatness unto our God!

Mugombe then read other passages from the Hebrew Bible that related to the festival, the season, or an event in the community. He concluded with a sermon, urging the community to strengthen itself through faith.

Mugombe and other members of the community questioned Oded intensively about Judaism and Jewish life, despite Oded's continued protests that he was not a rabbi or well versed in Jewish law. He did settle disputes between Mugombe and another community leader over which direction congregants should face during prayer and over the precise dates for celebrating Jewish festivals. Mugombe had correctly instructed the congregation to face north toward Jerusalem; his dates for the holidays, based on an old calendar supplied by David Solomon, were, according to Oded, "surprisingly accurate."

Oded found that closing the Jewish school had seriously weakened the community, and he wrote in a pamphlet published in 1973 that the Abayudaya desperately needed outside help:

In view of the Christian missionaries' vigorous activity and their great influence in Uganda, and as a result of their long-standing control of most of the schools and clinics (the system of state-controlled education is a recent introduction into Uganda), many of the children of the community became Christians while attending mission schools. This was the hardest blow for the Abayudaya and is responsible for the fact that the community has come to consist of elderly people, women and children; most of the youth of school-going age have abandoned the Jewish faith.

Oded also wrote articles about the Abayudaya for newspapers and magazines in Israel, England, and the United States. He found support for them from an organization called the World Union for the Propagation of Judaism. The group donated $100 to pay for a concrete floor for the crumbling synagogue, which had been built from cut tree limbs covered with plaster. The World Union at first tried—and failed—to recruit a rabbi to teach the Abayudaya, then planned to send one of the young Abayudaya to Israel to be trained in a *yeshiva*. Mugombe recommended Isaac Kakungulu, the founder's grandson, who was then a twenty-year-old teacher. After years in Christian schools, Isaac had only a vague knowledge of the Abayudaya religion, yet he was perhaps the only young person with an interest in reviving the community. The plan to train Isaac didn't materialize. By that time, Uganda had fallen into political turmoil and the government refused to let him leave the country. The Abayudaya were once again cut off from the world; any hope for revival would have to come from within.

Idi Amin seized power in Uganda in 1971 and soon began the brutal massacre of tens of thousands of his perceived enemies. He unofficially made Islam the state religion, although the majority of Ugandans remained Christians. In Mbale, local officials prohibited the Abayudaya from reading the Bible or conducting funeral services. "They just poured soil on you and buried you like a dead dog," Gershom recalls. The main synagogue on Nabugoye Hill, for which Oded had helped raise money, deteriorated. Yacob, one of the Abayudaya leaders, tried to save the sections of the tin roof from looters by taking them to another leader's house for safekeeping. A local police officer saw Yacob carrying the roof, charged him with stealing it, and brought him to prison, where he was held for three days. The police eventually believed his story and he was released.

During this era, local Muslims took over Gershom's father's land and destroyed his synagogue. Without the financial support of his congregation, his father had turned to farming, yet he continued to practice his beliefs. He invited Abayudaya elders to worship with him in his home on the Sabbath and holidays, and performed circumcisions in secret. He even built a booth to celebrate the fall harvest Festival of Sukkot and read the Bible there, despite the prohibition. When one of the village chiefs, a Muslim, visited and saw him with the Bible, he threatened to turn him over to the authorities. Gershom's father bribed him and escaped punishment.

Gershom was born in 1969, the second son from his father's second marriage. During Amin's rule, he received his primary education a few miles down the hill from Nabugoye, in a Christian primary school in Nankusi village. There were ten other Abayudaya in the school; most of the students and all of the teachers were Christians.

Each of the seven grades maintained a garden to help provide food for their teachers; the students were required to work in the gardens on Saturdays, the day of rest for the Abayudaya. Gershom's father had told his son that those who work on the Sabbath would be killed by the hand of God. Gershom came home from his first week in school fearing for his life. His father wisely modified his warning, telling him that God would not harm Jews who were ordered to work on the Sabbath but would punish those who forced them to do so. Gershom's father refused, however, to modify his opposition to mandatory Christian prayers. He petitioned the school officials and eventually received their assent to exempt his son and other Abayudaya from reciting the Hail Mary and other prayers each morning.

The Christian students resented this special treatment and derided the Abayudaya for being different. Every day before lunch, the classes came together to sing hymns and popular African songs. A small group of students gathered in a corner to sing their own composition, taunting and needling the Abayudaya:

The Abayudaya are bad,
All Jews are bad.
They caught Jesus
And put him on the cross.
Even when he cried
They did not have mercy.

The teachers pretended they didn't notice. Gershom and the other Abayudaya students, however, couldn't easily dismiss this daily ritual, the age-old libel that the Jews had killed Christ. They simmered with embarrassment and anger, yet they endured it silently. "Sometimes I would hate myself for being a Jew," Gershom says. "I didn't want to go back to school. But my father always encouraged me. He said we were God's chosen people, that He loves us more." Gershom became the top student in his school. His half brother Joab, who later became president of the community, was the star of the soccer team. "All the Abayudaya were the best in school," Gershom says, "the best athletes, singers, and students."

The Abayudaya quietly celebrated Amin's humiliation in 1976, when he assisted terrorists who had hijacked an Air France flight originating in Israel and forced it down in Entebbe. The hijackers demanded the release of imprisoned terrorists and threatened to kill more than 100 Jewish passengers after releasing the others. Amin at first pretended to befriend the hostages, but then he stationed his soldiers at the airport to help protect the terrorists. On July 4, Israeli troops staged a daring raid, killing all of the terrorists and several Ugandan soldiers. They rescued all but two of the hostages, who were killed during the attack.

Amin was overthrown nearly three years later, in the spring of 1979, close to the date on which the Abayudaya previously had celebrated Passover, the Feast of Freedom. Drums again called the Abayudaya to prayer, and like Jews in ancient times, they slaughtered a goat, gathered bitter herbs, and made their own *matzoh*. In what was left of the Nabugoye Hill synagogue, they read the story of Moses, Pharaoh, and the exodus from Egypt; drank wine; and recited prayers long into the night. After nearly ten years of practicing in secret, however, many of the elders had forgotten how to worship. A few weeks later, when one of the elders died, the Abayudaya held their first public funeral in nearly a decade. The elders argued with one another over proper rituals and prayers. Some of the non-Jews who attended the funeral laughed and made fun of the Abayudaya.

Gershom again felt embarrassed, this time by his own people. He had suffered years of taunting for being a Jew, yet his religion had become an empty shell. The Abayudaya had lost touch with many of their traditions, and after Gershom's father became ill, there was no one left who could teach them. Gershom and his classmates decided to teach themselves. In 1982, they formed the Young Jewish Club and studied the Hebrew alphabet books and prayer books Oded had helped get for them. Gershom's father predicted his son would become a rabbi.

During the rainy season, Gershom's father had slipped on his way to the garden and fractured his hip. Like Kakungulu, the founder of the Abayudaya, he refused medical treatment. He remained in bed for months. His health worsened as his family—two wives and nine children—struggled to find food during the famine and civil war of the mid-1980s. "We never had enough to eat," Gershom remembers. "My father always had been the one to cultivate the land." Gershom's father died in 1986.

"Life was not good for us then," Gershom says. "I felt I was on my own." He and his older brother, Aaron, skipped classes two days a week to maintain their garden and to work for others, planting and harvesting beans. His two sisters dropped out of school and got married; Joab dropped out to work on a farm full-time. Gershom's schoolwork suffered as he tried to make up for the missed classes; he also couldn't afford to pay his teachers for the private tutoring that was necessary to prepare for exams. Gershom and the other Abayudaya had little time for their religion. The Young Jewish Club stopped meeting.

By 1988, the community was so weak that the Anglican school once again saw an opportunity to claim ownership of

Nabugoye Hill. The authorities in nearby Mbale supported the school's claim. This time, the aged and dispirited Abayudaya elders did not resist. Their timidity, however, motivated Gershom and his classmates to form a new youth group. They called it the *kibbutz*, the Hebrew term for the communal settlements first founded by Zionist pioneers before the establishment of the State of Israel, and symbolic of the self-reliance and dedication of those early settlers.

"We were extremists, like militant Zionists," Gershom says. "Ndaula encouraged us, but Mugombe and the elders told us not to act. They believed we were risking our lives. It created a split between the youth and the elders. We told them they were our enemies now, and we were taking charge." Early one morning in the spring of 1988, just after the start of classes at the Christian primary school, Gershom and ten other young men climbed silently through the familiar bushes and up a rocky dirt path toward the school. Their fists and jaws were clenched, and their faces radiated with the intense stares of zealots, Gershom recalls. Although they planned for a long stay, they carried only guitars, drums, Bibles, and Hebrew lesson books. As the schoolchildren quieted down and the teachers began their lessons in a mud building nearby, the Abayudaya crept into the school staff house, a whitewashed building with a tin roof where a few staff members from the Christian school slept at night. Like 1960s student radicals taking over a university administration building, the young men began their peaceful occupation on Nabugoye Hill.

Once they had settled in, the young men spent their days reading and studying. Like ancient Jews who had been forced into exile by the Babylonians, they reinvented their Judaism. They composed new songs, based on African melodies, to the prayers and psalms. They pored over passages in the Bible, debating their meanings and questioning some of the practices handed down by the elders. Since Moses had removed his sandals in front of the Burning Bush, should Jews remove their shoes before entering the synagogue, or is this practice to be followed only by Muslims? What is the proper ritual for slaughtering meat and draining its blood? Are there restrictions on what women can do during their menstrual periods?

They ate simple meals of rice and beans and took turns visiting with their families at home. At night they slept on the floor of the sparsely furnished house while one of them guarded the door against the attack that was certain to come.

At first the school officials and local authorities chose not to confront them, assuming that the young people soon would tire of their sit-in. The officials visited the staff house and encouraged the Abayudaya to leave. After a week, the authorities began to lose patience and delivered a formal order to vacate. The occupiers ignored it. The following Saturday, local officials held a meeting near the staff house.

The mayor began by promising the school authorities and residents of the area around Nabugoye that they would have his full support in their efforts to take ownership of the land. Before the mayor could finish, Gershom and the other Abayudaya teenagers emerged from the staff house, playing their guitars and drums and singing loudly. "This is our land, the land of our forefathers," they chanted, "and we will never leave." They marched around and through the crowd, disrupting the meeting and forcing the mayor to cut short his speech. The next day, armed soldiers and police came to arrest them.

Four of the young men—including Gershom, his brothers Joab and Aaron, and a young man now named Ibrahim—were taken to a prison about three miles from Mbale. The guards told them to remove their shoes and shirts and pushed them inside a jail cell with twenty-five other prisoners. The four men knew they would be beaten. "We remembered the stories of Jewish martyrs who had been tortured for their faith," Gershom says. "We were prepared to die for our cause."

The other prisoners were ordered to discipline them. They made the four Abayudaya sit in a crouch while they slapped them, then made them punch the walls of the cell until their hands bled. The discipline lasted for two nights. During the day, all of the prisoners worked outside in a garden. They were given one meal a day, a small chunk of maize and uncooked beans, and slept on the floor at night. After their fourth day in jail, Isaac Kakungulu, who had become a lawyer after Ugandan authorities had prohibited him from leaving for Israel to study, represented them in court. Ibrahim's family helped them post bail, and they were released. They immediately rejoined the other youths in the staff house and continued their occupation.

Other members of the community rallied behind them. Parents with young daughters encouraged them to join the young men, hopeful that they would find Jewish husbands. That, too, was a success. Many of the married couples in the community today first met during the occupation. The growing group of young people sang, danced, and studied together as they planned to build a new synagogue on Nabugoye Hill.

Several years earlier, Joab had visited Nairobi, which is a twelve-hour ride from Mbale, and attended services at the synagogue there. His visit inspired the group to draw up plans for their own synagogue, although their resources were limited. They picked a site next to the staff house, the highest spot on Nabugoye Hill, with a wide view of the dense forest and banana groves below. It was to be a simple structure, perhaps not so different from the first synagogues built by Jews in the diaspora under Greek rule. They planned a one-story brick building with a concrete floor, about ten feet wide and fifty feet long. It would remain exposed to the sun and rain—the young people had no funds to buy doors, windows, or a roof. Following Jewish practice, it was to be a house of prayer, study, and assembly. They planned to build wooden benches along the walls, where community members could pray and gather for meetings, and school desks behind the pulpit, where children could study. They would leave an opening in the far wall, facing the pulpit, where they hoped some day to place a Torah.

Inside the staff house, they began to make bricks from straw and clay. By the end of the year, the bricks had filled the house, and they began to stack them outside. When the Anglican school headmaster confronted them, they told him they intended to donate the bricks to the school. It soon became apparent that they had lied. As the rainy season ended, the Abayudaya young people began to build their new synagogue on a barren hill in the shadow of Mt. Elgon.

By the time soldiers forcibly evicted them from the staff house in the spring of 1989, the young people were ready to move into the foundation of the new synagogue. They continued to study and pray as they stacked the brick walls, held to-gether by homemade mortar. They also began to build a small house across from the synagogue, which they would use as an office and residence.

Aaron Kintu Moses, Gershom's brother, visited Nairobi, seeking support to complete the synagogue. The members of the Jewish congregation there, mostly foreign diplomats and businessmen, seemed dismissive. But Douglas King, a visiting English Jew, was intrigued by Aaron's story and arranged to visit the Abayudaya in 1991. He later wrote an article about the community for Britain's *Jewish Chronicle.* The next year, Ger-shom attended Yom Kippur services in Nairobi and met two American college students, Matthew Meyer and Julia Chamovitz, who were doing volunteer work in Kenya. They ac-cepted Gershom's invitation to visit the Abayudaya.

After Meyer and Chamovitz's visit in November 1992, the Mbale authorities gave up their efforts to evict the Abayudaya, discouraged by their persistence and hopeful that the arrival of foreigners might contribute to Mbale's economy. It had taken nearly four years, but the young zealots had won their battle to retake Nabugoye Hill. Now, with Meyer's help, they sought outside support to revive their community.

When he returned to the United States, Matthew Meyer spoke to his congregation in Wilmington, Delaware, about his visit to the Abayudaya:

The *Shabbat* I spent with the Abayudaya community of Mbale, Uganda, a little over a month ago is one that has changed my life. . . . What both Julia and I saw was unquestionably a Jewish Friday-night service. The service itself was magical. Some English responsive reading, the *Shema*— a Friday-night service like at any other synagogue except for the fact this one happened to be in a mud hut with the Ten Commandments and pictures of the Torah chalked in on the walls.

Meyer gave more speeches about the Abayudaya and raised funds at his Hillel at Brown University so they could buy timber and iron for a roof. He also solicited help from Kulanu, a nonprofit group based in Maryland. In June 1995, Kulanu sent a fifteen-member delegation to meet the Abayudaya, led by Rabbi Jacques Cukierkorn, who at the time headed a congregation in Alexandria, Virginia. The evening they arrived, more than 100 members of the Abayudaya community greeted them with cheers, clapping, and high-pitched shrieks of delight. The visitors joined them in singing Israeli folk songs. The following day, a choir entertained the delegation with a welcome song and an English rendition of the Twenty-third Psalm, accompanied by a drum and guitar. The community also conducted a mock Sabbath service—it was a Thursday—so the Kulanu members could film it. The delegation talked for hours with members of the community about Jewish practice and the history of the Abayudaya. They agreed to make arrangements for an Orthodox rabbi to visit.

Kulanu brought more attention to the Abayudaya. "They are very, very committed to this religion that they have adopted," Rabbi Cukierkorn told National Public Radio's Robert Siegel, who was a member of his congregation in Alexandria. "One of

the reasons they want to be Jewish is because God loves oppressed people. They want to have a special relationship with
God. For me, it was very moving, a very, very spiritual experience because everything that we have and we take for granted
they challenge so much."

Following Kulanu's visit, Matt Meyer set up an Abayudaya
Web page, featuring pictures of members of the community in
front of their new synagogue, a brief history of the Abayudaya,
and recordings of their music. Kulanu published dozens of articles about the Abayudaya in their newsletter, established an education fund for the young people, and helped them raise
additional funds by selling their knitted skullcaps and recordings
of their music by mail.

J. Hershy Worch, an Orthodox rabbi, later visited at Kulanu's request to teach the Abayudaya more about Jewish law.
Rabbi Worch tried to help them rebuild the *mikvah* (ritual bath)
that Kakungulu had used for conversions, and instructed them
in the proper use of it as part of the monthly purification ritual for women. He watched and commented as Gershom
slaughtered a chicken, and reviewed the proper method of circumcision with him.

Rabbi Worch also brought the Abayudaya a present from Kulanu, a Torah scroll donated by a congregation from Auburn,
Maine. He insisted, however, that the Torah was a loan, not a
gift, because the Abayudaya were not officially Jews. The borrowed parchment now sits behind the white curtain facing the
pulpit in the synagogue on Nabugoye Hill.

The connection to Kulanu has brought the Abayudaya visitors and support from around the world, but the Abayudaya

have not yet fulfilled Kakungulu's dream of being accepted as Jews.

"I'm not sure it's a good analogy, but being Jewish is like being a member of the Rotary," Rabbi Cukierkorn said in the radio interview. "You can like the Rotary Club, you can live by Rotary values, and, you know, you can even try to sneak into the meetings. But unless you are a real member and the other members accept you as such, you're not a real Rotarian."

Gershom, his wife, Zipporah, and their two children are now among the handful of Abayudaya who are permanent residents of Nabugoye. Relations with the non-Abayudaya neighbors, as well as with the Christian primary school, are peaceful, however. Gershom earns his living as a part-time teacher at a boys' school about ten miles away. He occasionally volunteers to tutor some of the non-Jewish children in the area for their school examinations, the same preparation he was unable to afford when he was younger.

The Christian primary school still leases much of the land on Nabugoye Hill, and many Abayudaya children are enrolled there. It occupies two rundown buildings made of cut tree branches lashed together and plastered with mud. A frame for a new school building is nearly completed. The children, dressed in white shirts and blue pants or skirts, sit cross-legged on the dirt floors, closely attentive to their teachers. In the afternoons, they run races or play soccer with a ball made of rags in a large, open field as skinny cows chew on grass near the makeshift goals.

Gershom now walks easily through the school area and jokes playfully with the teachers he once saw as his enemies. He occasionally chides the schoolchildren when they play too loudly. There is only one visible sign of the 1988 conflict with the school. Across from the staff house and the new synagogue, on the wooden door of the brick building that serves as the Abayudaya office and Gershom's home, are three words that were scrawled in chalk a year earlier: "Ninth *Kibbutz* Anniversary."

The site of Kakungulu's original synagogue is on the other side of the soccer field, a bare patch of ground surrounded by large rocks. Just beyond it are a new brick building and the foundation for a second one. It is here that Gershom plans to revive Kakungulu's dream for a Jewish school.

The community has completed one building with Kulanu's help, and Gershom has applied for grants to complete the other. They would house a primary school, which would be supported by the government, and a secondary school, which would charge tuition. Poor children and orphans would attend for free. Malaria, tuberculosis, and AIDS, which have killed hundreds of thousands throughout Africa, have decimated the Abayudaya as well. There are about fifty Abayudaya children without parents.

The schools would offer basic education as well as vocational courses in woodworking, computer studies, music, dance, drama, tailoring, shoemaking, bricklaying, and needlework, Gershom says. And they would offer Jewish education—instead of lessons in Christianity or Islam—as one of their electives. The schools would provide teaching jobs for Abayudaya who have attended university—Gershom has completed his studies at the Islamic University, and his brother Aaron is studying for a business degree in Kampala—and tuition revenue that could be used to support other Abayudaya who plan to enroll in a university.

Gershom's hope for the future of his community lies within the walls of these two small buildings.

It's about a ten-minute walk downhill, through bushes and over boulders and brush, from the new school buildings to the community *mikvah*. It was designed so that water from a nearby spring would flow into the small cement pool. The pool is about four feet deep, with steps leading down to it, and is partially secluded by waist-high reeds. The water is murky and infested with snails; Gershom says they hope to clean it so the women can use it for their monthly purification ritual after each menstrual cycle. Naome Kintu Moses, who had accompanied us down the hill, explains that Rabbi Worch had instructed the women in the laws of ritual purity.

Under Orthodox law, a woman is considered to be *niddah*—an excluded person—during her menstrual period, and both she and her husband are prohibited from having sexual relations. As with many of their practices, the Abayudaya have added their own interpretation to Jewish ritual. Naome says she and the other women cannot visit the synagogue during their menstrual periods, based on practices followed in some Jewish communities.

Naome is the head of the Abayudaya Women's Association, which was formed in 1995 after Kulanu's visit. Its goal is to help the Abayudaya women further their education and gain more voice in the community. The Heifer Project, a nonprofit agency based in Arkansas that supplies cattle to women in the Third World to help them become self-sufficient, plans to send them heifers so they can produce milk and raise calves.

"Men make the choices," Naome says. "That's the way it is

in Africa." Men also control the Abayudaya; all the elected officers are male. "Men are always dominant in the community," she says. "Women don't have enough education to have a voice." Naome and several other young women, including Gershom's wife, Zipporah, have returned to complete secondary school with tuition assistance from Kulanu.

"Women should not remain behind all the time," Naome says. "Women and men should be on the same level. The girls have always been first in primary school. We now have a woman vice president in Uganda, and laws prohibiting spousal abuse. Even in the villages now there is no abuse, no beating. Men's powers are decreasing." Naome says she plans to become an accountant or a secretary once she finishes school, and to run for president of the Abayudaya community. She hopes her daughter, Simcha, can grow up to become a lawyer.

A bit farther down the hill, Gershom points out a new brick building that the Abayudaya recently completed, except for the roof. They plan to use it as a guest house. The spring that feeds the *mikvah* will supply it with fresh water, and nearby utility poles will supply power. Only a handful of homes in the area have electricity. It is also near a dirt road that leads to Mbale. A visiting geneticist—no one seemed to know what he hoped to find, since the Abayudaya have no genetic links to other Jews—donated the funds for the guest house.

In their first seventy years, there were perhaps eight or nine foreign visitors to the Abayudaya community. It is still far too remote to become a major attraction, but new visitors—doctors, anthropology students, and curious tourists—now arrive regularly. Like the earliest visitors, they have brought funds for the community and new ideas about Judaism. Inevitably, the foreigners will have an influence on the Abayudaya. But Gershom, like Kakungulu before him, isn't worried that the community might lose its unique identity.

"We tend to adopt new things and add to what we already have," Gershom says. "We don't want to be different from other Jews. We already are different from other people."

Later that afternoon, Gershom and Zipporah begin to prepare dinner as their two young children, Igaal and Daffna, play in the dirt around the office and synagogue. Gershom starts a wood fire in an open hut behind the staff house, while Zipporah fetches water from a stream and walks up the hill with heavy jugs balanced on her head.

Zipporah grew up near Samson Mugombe's village. She was only ten years old when she met Gershom, during the occupation of Nabugoye Hill. They were married five years later in traditional village style. Gershom brought gifts to her family, they accepted his proposal of marriage, and the two of them began to live together. Igaal was born a year later, and Daffna two years after that.

Daffna had been a twin, but her sibling died moments after she was born. As Gershom and the doctors struggled to save her sibling—like most of the young Abayudaya, Gershom accepts modern medicine—they left Daffna wrapped in blankets on a nearby table. A hospital worker accidentally knocked her from the table. Gershom leaped across the room and caught her just before she hit the floor. A year later, when Matt Meyer was visiting, Daffna was badly scalded by hot water boiling in a pot over the kitchen fire. While they were treating her in the hospital, she contracted measles and suffered severe abscesses from the intravenous needles. After all she has survived, Gershom says, he thinks Daffna will live a long life. At her second birthday party, Gershom recites the *Shehecheyanu*, the Hebrew prayer for new occasions, thanking God for "keeping us alive, sustaining us, and allowing us to reach this season."

In the darkness that evening, Zipporah catches one of their chickens roaming in the bushes near their house and the synagogue. She holds it close to her and strokes it gently as she brings it to Gershom. The chicken seems peaceful in her arms and makes no sound as Gershom quickly and skillfully cuts its neck. Based on the ritual Rabbi Worch taught them, they drain the blood, pluck the feathers, and soak the bird in water, making certain all the blood is removed. Then Zipporah cooks the chicken slowly in a pan over the wood fire, along with pots of maize and rice, and serves dinner under the stars on Nabugoye Hill.

THERE ARE STILL four Abayudaya communities, as there were in Kakungulu's day, spread over a wide area. Gershom estimates that there are now 500 to 600 Abayudaya, but perhaps only 200 are active in the synagogues and communities. Gershom serves as the spiritual leader in Nabugoye, where the Abayudaya from the other three communities come for major holidays and meetings. The communities have elected central leaders—Gershom's half brother Joab is president, and his brother Aaron is secretary—who manage finances for all of the Abayudaya. The leaders walk or bicycle the two miles to

Mbale to use the bank, post office, and public fax. The city center looks like a set for a Wild West movie, with wide dirt streets, raised wooden sidewalks, and unpainted wood storefronts with plate-glass windows. A sign in the window of the meat store promises, "Scale cheaters don't exist here."

The other communities have their own leaders as well, who are sometimes at odds with the central leadership. Each synagogue has maintained its own practices. The nearest Abayudaya community to Nabugoye is in the village of Namanyoyi, separated by about three miles of rocks, bushes, fields, banana groves, and grazing goats and turkeys. It is led by Samson Mugombe, the last surviving teacher trained by Kakungulu. He lives in a two-room hut with a Star of David and Hanukkah *menorah* painted on either side of the entrance. A Hanukkah card is attached to the door, beneath the words *Samson's House.* Samson moves slowly, supporting himself with a long thick pole as he steps down from the threshold and struggles to sit on a small wooden stool outside in the shade. His mind is still sharp.

When he was a teenager, Samson says, Kakungulu trained him to serve as a teacher in the Palissa district and to beat a drum to call people to services. Samson still conducts services in his synagogue, a tiny mud hut. He has preserved the old ways for his small, elderly congregation; the service remains much the way it was in Kakungulu's time and when Oded visited in the 1960s. A few things have changed, however. Samson no longer baptizes boys in the ritual bath after their circumcisions, and with Gershom's encouragement, he has added other readings from the Bible to his services. Gershom and Samson have mended their relationship since the days of the *kib-*

butz and now have friendly arguments over which prayers and rituals to change or maintain.

Palissa, where Samson and most of Kakungulu's earliest followers grew up, is the largest of the four communities, with two synagogues and an active youth group. It is about five miles south of Nabugoye, not far from a newly paved highway.

The main synagogue in Palissa is less than half the size of the Nabugoye synagogue. It is made mostly of mud and crude bricks and has a dirt floor. There is a recession in the front wall for a Torah, but it contains only a chalk drawing of two tablets with Hebrew letters, representing the Ten Commandments. The chairman of the youth group is a tall, serious young man named Enosh Keki, Joab's nephew. His classmates call him "the rabbi."

"Our rabbi died a few years ago, so we don't have a rabbi," Enosh says. "Members of the community feel I should take over. But I feel I have much to learn about Jewish life and how to have a Jewish home."

Enosh sits on one of the long, low wooden benches as the women gather at the front of the synagogue to sing Jewish and Luganda songs. Then the vice chairman of the community speaks at length about Palissa's need for money, a new synagogue, office space, medical care, education, and oxen. He complains that all the resources and attention are going to the leadership at Nabugoye and that little assistance has reached Palissa.

The Abayudaya's only Jewish cemetery is a short walk from the Palissa synagogue. The rabbi's widow lives nearby, a frail old woman with close-cropped white hair who is wearing a black-

and-yellow robe emblazoned with a Pittsburgh Steelers emblem. Most Abayudaya are still buried next to their homes; the rabbi and several others were buried in the new cemetery based on Rabbi Worch's instructions. A *chevra kadisha*—Jewish burial society—washes the bodies, wraps them in linen shrouds, and buries them within twenty-four hours of their death. The flat slabs of stone over each grave are chiseled with Stars of David.

I RETURN TO Nabugoye for my second Friday-night service with the Abayudaya. Aaron, Naome's husband and Gershom's brother, is going to lead the service, and he asks me if I would be willing to discuss the week's Torah portion. There actually are two portions for the week, *Vayakhel* and *Parah,* which is added in preparation for Passover. *Parah* is far more interesting but nearly impenetrable. It is the story of the red cow.

In Numbers 19, God calls on Moses to find an unblemished red heifer that has never been yoked, and to take it to a priest to slaughter and burn it. The ashes are to be set aside and used to purify any among the Children of Israel who make contact with a dead body. Yet the ashes themselves are impure—anyone who touches them will become temporarily unclean. This paradox—that which purifies also contaminates—has troubled scholars for millennia. Even King Solomon, the commentaries state, was unable to understand it.

I have less than an hour to read the passages and prepare my sermon. I sit in the office, squinting at the text and commentaries as darkness once again surrounds Nabugoye Hill. Then I walk toward the sounds of *Lecha Dodi,* welcoming the Sabbath queen, as I had a week earlier the first time I entered the synagogue.

We share wine and *challah* and sing psalms before Aaron invites me to talk. I begin by thanking the Abayudaya for their week of hospitality, for inviting me into their homes and sharing their food. Their devotion to Judaism, despite their hardships, I say, makes me proud to be a Jew. Now, however, I face a humbling task, trying to explain the story of the red heifer. Some have suggested that the red heifer was part of an atonement for the Israelites' sin of making the golden calf. More recently, an ultra-Orthodox sect has claimed that the birth of a red heifer in Israel foreshadows the construction of the Third Temple in Jerusalem. In my view, I say, the passage implies that much about God and the Torah are beyond human understanding. To me, it seems a reminder of our own limitations.

ON MY LAST day with the Abayudaya, Aaron, Naome, Simcha, and I hire a taxi to visit Namutumba, the most remote Abayudaya community, more than an hour south of Mbale. The village is located off the main highway, along a dirt road.

The chairman of the Namutumba community lives in a small hut in a clearing about a half mile down the dirt road. He stands stiffly beside his wife and eldest son as he explains the current state of the community. There are now about seventy members of the community, he says, most of them young people. They built a new synagogue several years ago but it collapsed in the heavy rains last fall. The Seventh Day Adventist Church has since purchased the land where the synagogue once stood. He says he offered his own land for a new synagogue but argued with the rabbi over a fair price. For now, the rabbi, who lives in an even more remote area, is holding services each Sabbath in a different family's home. The chairman says he doesn't know where to find him.

We get back in the taxi with the chairman's eldest son, Reuven, who calls out directions. The road beyond the chairman's house wends through high grass and around trees and bushes; the deep ruts make the road almost impassable in a car. Each turn in what remains of the road seems to lead deeper into the bush. After ten minutes of bouncing and scraping, the taxi reaches another clearing and comes to a stop. This is the rabbi's home, Reuven says, and perhaps his wife can tell us where he is holding services today. A *menorah* is painted in white by the door, and a Jewish prayer shawl is visible inside the thatched-roof hut. To Reuven's surprise, the rabbi emerges, wearing one of the Abayudaya skullcaps, a knitted red cap decorated with *menorahs*. The rabbi, Eli Kagwa, explains that his daughter is sick and he has stayed home this Sabbath to help care for her.

Eli says he was born in Namutumba but grew up in Mbale, where he studied and learned to pray with the help of Samson Mugombe. He spent twenty-five years in the army, then returned to Namutumba in 1992. Two years later, the old rabbi died and Eli took over. There was no leadership, he says, and he hopes to revitalize Judaism in the community and conduct Sabbath services. Eli says the community paid the chairman for some of his land to build a new synagogue, but he wants more money. Eli has lost confidence in him. Recently, Eli donated some of his own land and began building a synagogue.

As he walks through the brush toward the synagogue, Eli explains that he teaches a Torah class for about forty young people each week. After class, they work together on the synagogue. In a field of tall, dried grass, Eli proudly points out the completed frame, a rectangle of tall, two-inch-thick tree branches connected to a peaked roof also made of branches. Eli says he hopes to have a thatched roof completed within a month and is making bricks so the walls of the synagogue can be more permanent. Aaron promises to return and help the students learn more about Jewish prayers and traditions.

We walk back to his house, where his wife lays out a blanket, and Eli brings out a prayer book and puts on his prayer shawl. In this remote clearing, surrounded by banana trees and the sounds of birds and crickets, he offers blessings for the Torah and for his country. The blessings are familiar, but this brief Sabbath service seems only vaguely connected to the Orthodox and Conservative liturgies with which I grew up. Yet it would be presumptuous for me to question Eli or to add my own prayers. Even in this most isolated outpost of Uganda's self-proclaimed Jews, I feel I am witnessing a new spark of Jewish life, true to the spirit and tradition that has reshaped Judaism for thousands of years.

. . . Semei Kakungulu was a mythic figure . . . There he established a new sect, "the community of Jews (Abayudaya) who trust in the Lord." Michael Twaddle, *Kakungulu and the Creation of Uganda, 1868–1928* (Athens, OH: Ohio University Press, 1993), pp. 1, 5–7, 15–28, 183–90, 225–26, 265–88.

The original Beta Israel . . .   Nathan Schur, *History of the Karaites* (New York: Verlag Peter Lang GmbH, 1992), p. 154.

The Lemba in southern Africa . . .   Nicholas Wade, "DNA Backs a Tribe's Tradition of Early Descent from the Jews," *New York Times,* May 9, 1999, p. A1; NOVA Online, "Tudor Parfitt's Remarkable Journey" <http://www.pbs.org/wgbh/nova/israel/parfitt.html>.

Geneticists have found . . .   Public Broadcasting Service, "Lost Tribes of Israel," NOVA #2706, broadcast February 22, 2000.

. . . an ill-fated plan to establish a Jewish homeland . . .   Desmond Stewart, *Theodor Herzl* (New York: Doubleday, 1974).

Kakungulu's new religion was an evangelical . . .   Arye Oded, "The Bayudaya: A Community of African Jews in Uganda," Shiloah Center for Middle Eastern and African Studies, Tel Aviv University, Tel Aviv, 1973.

What makes the Abayudaya unique . . .   I am indebted to Lee Malcus, a graduate student in anthropology at Boston University, for this insight.

Following Joseph's visit . . . Mugombe had correctly instructed the congregation . . .   Twaddle, *Kagungulu and the Creation of Uganda*; Oded, "The Bayudaya."

After Meyer and Chamovitz's visit . . .   Matt Meyer, "Excerpts from My Journal," and "A Speech I Gave to Beth Shalom, Wilmington, Delaware," The Abayudaya of Uganda <http://www-personal.umich.edu/~meyerm/Abayudaya>.

Rabbi Cukierkorn told National Public Radio's . . .   Robert Siegel, "All Things Considered," National Public Radio, August 3, 1995, transcript #1928-13.

Chapter Two

CHILDREN OF MOSES
AND ABRAHAM

Rosa Valderrama kneels on the stone slab, slowly carving letters with a small metal tool. A mason has made two stones earlier in the day, one to rest on top of the grave, and the other, engraved with a Star of David, to be placed perpendicular to it. The cement is still soft. Rosa chisels Hilda Raza's Hebrew name and her dates of birth and death on the vertical stone, below the star. Hilda died from an infection just a month ago, at age fifty-one. Her widower, Yishay Raza, and his friend, Próspero Luján, help Rosa use a ruler to keep the letters straight and evenly spaced. As the afternoon light fades over the city of Trujillo below us, Rosa sends a young boy to buy a candle at a small store in the nearby village. When he returns, Yishay lights the candle and sets it in melted wax on the concrete slab; I do my best to block the flame from the chilly wind blowing down from the barren foothills of the Andes behind us.

The cemetery where Hilda is buried sits on a remote hillside in the outskirts of Trujillo, Peru. A white-and-yellow stone arch identifies it as the St. John the Baptist cemetery. A huge stone cross, perhaps thirty feet high, stands in the center. Hundreds of simple graves, some next to tiny wooden houses that contain icons and blessings, surround it. Flowering cactus plants decorate most of the gravesites; nothing else grows in the powdery, gray soil. Each grave—except for the two beside us, one for Hilda and the other for Rosa's aunt Francisca, who died three months earlier—is marked with a wooden or stone cross.

The handful of families that has been visiting other graves departs as the sun sets. In the enveloping darkness, I can see the city lights flicker through the purple-gray haze, and the outline of the ocean to the west. Rosa now begins to carve Hilda's name and eulogy in Spanish in the horizontal stone as Yishay, Próspero, and I huddle around her. A barefoot cemetery worker, wearing a pink Arrowsmith cap, joins us. He squints at the letters Rosa has drawn earlier.

"What language is that?" he asks.

"It's Chinese," Rosa replies, half in jest and half to discourage rumors.

The story she conceals began in the mountains six decades ago, among a group of Peruvian peasants with unusual names who studied the Hebrew Bible, observed the practices of the ancient Hebrews, and retreated for a time into the Amazon jungle. Visitors came to teach them this strange language and other rituals. Later, bearded men in skullcaps came to test them and immerse them in the Moche river. Then most of them flew across the ocean to live in a desolate land west of the Jordan river, where the biblical prophets are buried. It is a tale as fabulous as any told by Gabriel García Márquez or Isabel Allende.

CAJAMARCA LIES ABOUT seventy miles northeast of Trujillo, in a fertile mountain valley. A huge cathedral dominates the center of town, surrounded by eucalyptus trees and large houses with red-tiled roofs. Not far from here, Spanish conquistadors first encountered the Incas, massacred thousands of them, and kidnapped their ruler, Atahualpa.

Segundo Villanueva was born in 1927 in Celendin, a village near Cajamarca, the eldest of five children of a poor peasant farmer. Like nearly everyone in the valley, he was raised as a Catholic and regularly attended church. When he was twelve, his father died suddenly, leaving him as head of the household. He and his younger brother, Álvaro, supported the family by planting crops and finding odd jobs in a nearby village; he also trained to be a carpenter. Villanueva's inheritance was his father's most precious possession: a Spanish translation of the Bible.

"I never had any problem with Catholicism," recalls Villanueva, a thin man with slightly hunched shoulders and a somber appearance. "I never knew anything else. But I started reading the Old Testament my father had left me with great enthusiasm and gradually saw another path. No one taught it to me; I learned it myself. I stopped going to church and studied at home. From reading the Bible, I came to the conclusion that the practices of the Hebrews were the only way; there was no other way."

Villanueva, who now lives in Kfar Tapuach in Israel's West Bank, read and reread the stories of the Hebrews and their leaders, from Abraham making his covenant with God to Moses receiving God's laws on Mt. Sinai. He was particularly moved by the majesty and poetry of the Book of Psalms. The words of Psalm 121 seemed to have a special meaning for a young man who grew up in a mountain valley:

I will lift up mine eyes unto the mountains:
From whence shall my help come?
My help cometh from the Lord,
Who made heaven and earth.

He will not suffer thy foot to be moved;
He that keepeth thee will not slumber.
Behold, He that keepeth Israel
Doth neither slumber nor sleep.

To Villanueva, these words showed that the people of Israel have a special relationship with God. Their ways, it seemed to him, are the only true path to reach God. Though he could not explain the powerful force that drew him to the ancient Hebrews, he shared his vision with his family and friends, who joined him in studying the Bible.

Villanueva and the others made Saturday, the seventh day, their day of rest. For several years, they worshiped together with a group of vegetarian Seventh Day Adventists but eventually abandoned all Christian practices. Villanueva's followers began to pray together in his home each Saturday and Jewish holiday and to study the Bible from sunrise to sunset. They found inspiration from the Book of Psalms, and guidance for their practices in the Book of Leviticus.

"The men didn't work in the fields, and the women didn't light fires or cook on the Sabbath," says Villanueva. "We celebrated Passover, the Festival of Weeks [Shavuot], the Day of Atonement, and the Festival of Booths [Sukkot], all the holidays in the Bible. We separated our animals—we divided those the Bible describes as unclean, such as pigs, from the cows and sheep."

Villanueva knew only one Jew, a young man from Cajamarca named Jose Goldstein whose family had emigrated from Germany and knew little about Judaism. One Passover, Villanueva invited Goldstein to his home to celebrate. Villanueva and his followers read the story of the exodus from Egypt and commemorated the holiday with unleavened bread, wine, and songs. As the evening ended, Goldstein was overcome with emotion.

"I don't know any of these rituals," Goldstein said, choking back tears. "You're more Jewish than I am."

Villanueva moved to Trujillo, Peru's third largest city, in the 1950s so that his eldest son could attend school there. Most of his followers came with him, although a few continued with their own congregation in Cajamarca. Villanueva made a modest living building wooden furniture. The sugar industry, most of which was controlled by foreign companies, dominated Trujillo's economy. The city was known also as a hotbed for radical, anti-imperialist politics and opposition to the Catholic church, making it a relatively safe haven for Villanueva and his followers.

"Anyone who wanted to study Hebrew practices could join us," Villanueva recalls. "As long as you kept studying, you were a member. When we prayed, the women sat apart from the men. We gave our children names from the Bible. We used a small room in my house for worship services, and I built a *mikvah* nearby."

Villanueva called the group Israel de Dios, or Israel of God. By the 1960s, there were more than forty congregants. Most came from poor Catholic families whose ancestry was a mix of Europeans and Indians. They were attracted by Villanueva's charisma and passion, although many had additional motivations for abandoning the church. Hernán Valderrama joined as a young man after a priest in Cajamarca took him to a soccer game and tried to molest him. Other members traced their ancestry to Marranos, Iberian Jews who were forced to convert to Catholicism during the Inquisition but continued to practice Jewish rituals in secret. Among them was Próspero Luján, a farmer and peddler who became president of the congregation after Villanueva left for Israel.

Próspero was born in 1932 in Lluin, a mountain village northeast of Trujillo, and baptized in the local church. When he was eight years old and visiting his grandmother, he saw his uncle Anselmo smash a statue of San Isidro, the patron saint of farmers.

"Anselmo smiled at me and danced on the shards," says Próspero, a square-jawed man with a white goatee and deep-set eyes. "Anselmo said, 'This is no good.' Then he tore down pictures of Jesus and the saints throughout the house.

"Anselmo was a serious man. He was mayor of Lluin and intimidated nearly everyone. He stayed home to read the Hebrew Bible every Saturday, his day of rest. He told me that he was descended from Marranos from a small village in Spain, that he believed in one God, and that all idols were worthless."

Inspired by his uncle's passionate hatred of statues, Próspero began to read the Hebrew Bible every Saturday, impressed especially by the story of Moses smashing the golden calf and other passages demonstrating God's command to reject graven images. After he returned home from military service at age twenty-one, he went with his brother-in-law to a small church in the mountains, two miles from his home, to start his own crusade against idols.

"The church was empty when we arrived on Saturday morning," Próspero remembers. "The sanctuary was simple, decorated only by a small carving of Jesus on the cross and a picture of Mary. I found several two-foot-high statues, including San Isidro, in the loft. As I stared at these saints, they made me angry. 'These statues are false,' I told my brother-in-law. 'People should not worship them.' "

He pulled a hammer from his belt and swung it forcefully at San Isidro's neck, cleanly separating the head from the statue. It flew across the loft, then clattered noisily to the wooden floor. Próspero and his brother-in-law stood in silence for a few seconds, fearing that the priest had heard the sound from his house, only yards from the church. Then Próspero picked up the head of the statue, placed it in a cloth bag, and ran out of the church.

"When I got home, I smashed the bag against the floor until the statue's head was shattered into tiny pieces," Próspero says. "Like my uncle, I danced over the remains of San Isidro."

He returned to the same church several times, occasionally paying one of his friends to join him. On each visit, he decapitated another statue and brought the head home to shatter it and celebrate. The church soon hired a guard to protect it from the mysterious vandals. Próspero and his friends continued to go there, waiting in the woods nearby until the guard left for lunch. Over the following years, Próspero destroyed dozens of statues in small churches in his province.

"My greatest ambition was to destroy the giant statue of the Virgin that stood on a hill overlooking Otusco," Próspero says, "but I never got the chance. I tried once, but a priest wrestled with me and stopped me before I could do it."

Próspero's business often took him to Trujillo, where he sold fruits and vegetables. It was there that he learned of Israel de Dios and met Segundo Villanueva. Próspero attended services one Saturday and soon recognized a kinship between his beliefs and Villanueva's. Both of them rejected the divinity of Jesus and despised idol worship. Próspero became a loyal member of Israel de Dios. He now lives in Trujillo, where he is a member of the small Jewish congregation and runs a beverage delivery service from the first floor of his home. Yishay Raza has succeeded him as president of the congregation.

VILLANUEVA'S MOVEMENT WAS born in Cajamarca and Trujillo, but it reached maturity in the Amazon rain forest. In the 1960s, the Peruvian government promoted development of the Amazon by exempting new settlers from taxes. Many of the settlers were members of religious sects.

At the time, dozens of evangelical movements were rapidly gaining popularity, encroaching on nearly four centuries of Catholic dominance in Peru. Protestantism first arrived late in the nineteenth century. By the 1960s, there were congregations of Baptists, Pentecostals, Presbyterians, Seventh Day Adventists, and the Evangelical Church of Peru. Many of the newer sects took advantage of the reforms to claim land and test their followers' loyalty in the isolation of the jungle.

Some of the sects blended Indian beliefs and practices with Christianity; a few followed practices spelled out in the Hebrew Bible. Perhaps the strangest of these sects was the Israelite Mission of the New Universal Pact, founded by a messianic leader, Ezequiel Ataucusi Gamonal, who declared himself God's representative on earth. His movement attracted tens of thousands of followers throughout the country and established settlements in the Amazon bordering Brazil. Its members imitated the rituals of the ancient Hebrews as recorded in the Bible. The men grew long hair and beards and wore caps and tunics; the women wore dark clothes and veils. In 1995, Ataucusi, along with a Peruvian congressman who was a member, was accused of ordering the killing of fifteen dissident members of the sect. The chief of the Judicial Office of Internal Control told the Lima newspaper *La Republica* that four judges later released Ataucusi "in exchange for a bribe."

SHORTLY AFTER THE Six-Day War in Israel in 1967, Villanueva took nineteen families with him into the interior, not far from Iquitos, where tributaries from the Andes feed the

Amazon river. They were granted a large tract of land on the edge of the jungle, which they divided among the families. It was peaceful and isolated; the only threats came from poisonous snakes that hid in trees and bushes. They called it Hebrón.

"It was like a *kibbutz*," Villanueva recalls. "We did our own schooling for the younger children. Each family cleared its own land and grew what they could, bananas, cocoa, coffee, and corn. The land was very productive."

Settlers from other sects that had colonized the jungle, including Seventh Day Adventists, occasionally visited Villanueva and his followers and tried to convert them. Villanueva listened patiently but was usually disappointed by their lack of knowledge.

"We felt our reading of the Bible was superior," Villanueva says. "We followed the word. They all had their own interpretations but it was not the Bible itself. The Bible guided us perfectly. We didn't need any other direction."

There was one insight the others had to offer, however. They called Villanueva's followers Israelitas, the Spanish word for Jews. It was a label Villanueva accepted, although he knew little firsthand about how Jews practice their religion. He and his brother, Álvaro, decided to set out for Lima to learn more.

European Jews, including industrialists, bankers, merchants, and engineers, first had settled in Lima in the middle of the nineteenth century and established a Jewish cemetery. Nearly all of them intermarried and assimilated into Peruvian society in little more than a generation. The next wave of Jewish immigration came from Poland, Russia, and the Balkans at the end of the nineteenth century. Most initially made their living as peddlers, selling goods in cities and towns in the mountains and on the coast, and eventually setting up small businesses and cafés. Some Moroccan Jews settled in the Peruvian Amazon at about the same time. At the beginning of the twentieth century, there were synagogues in places like Trujillo and Iquitos. Another wave of Jewish immigrants arrived from Germany in the 1930s, and most of them settled in Lima. The small Jewish communities in the provinces eventually disappeared through intermarriage.

By the time the Villanueva brothers visited in 1970, nearly all of Peru's 5,000 Jews lived in Lima. They supported three congregations: a Conservative synagogue made up primarily of German immigrants; an Orthodox synagogue for the Eastern European Jews; and a congregation of Sephardic Jews originally from Morocco, who prayed in a room in the Orthodox synagogue. The community also had its own school, the Colegio León Pinelo, named for a Marrano whose grandfather was burned at the stake. Ninety-five percent of Lima's Jewish children attended it.

The Villanueva brothers visited all three synagogues. The only Jewish leader who met with them was Abraham ben Hamu, the rabbi of the Sephardic synagogue. Rabbi Hamu was fascinated with these strange men from the jungle, and he agreed to help them. He loaned them a copy of a Hebrew and Spanish prayer book as well as several books about Jewish practices and customs. The books provided details about each of the major Jewish holidays as well as commentaries from Maimonides and other rabbis and philosophers. The Villanueva brothers found a great deal in common between Israel de Dios and Judaism.

"We returned to the jungle and studied the books very carefully," Villanueva says. "But there was nothing except the prayer books which we didn't have before. The only major difference was that we didn't have circumcision."

Rabbi Hamu had told them that if they wished to follow the instructions of the Hebrew Bible scrupulously, the men would have to be circumcised. Villanueva agreed. With the rabbi's help, he eventually found a Jewish physician from Lima, Dr. Ruben Kogan, who was willing to perform circumcisions on non-Jews. Villanueva and his brother returned to Lima, where Dr. Kogan circumcised them.

Villanueva encouraged his other male followers to visit Dr. Kogan as well. Many of them resisted, for the first time challenging Villanueva's leadership. It divided the congregation, and a number of families decided to leave. Those who remained agreed it was time to abandon their colony in the jungle. In 1971, Villanueva and most of the remaining congregants returned to Trujillo; his brother, Álvaro, moved to Lima and established a new congregation there. Three families decided to remain in the jungle.

Both brothers continued to seek help from Rabbi Hamu and other Jews they had met in Lima. Villanueva also tried to enroll his ten-year-old son, whom he had named Joshua, in the Jewish school in Lima, but his application was rejected. The rabbis who ran the school told Villanueva his son could not attend because he was not Jewish. Joshua's rejection helped convince Villanueva that his congregation should not only follow the practices of Jews but also be accepted as Jews. It was an ambitious goal, particularly in a country where wealthy white men dominated the Jewish establishment and looked down on peasants like Villanueva.

Rabbi Hamu, from a Moroccan immigrant family, was more accommodating. He agreed to tutor Joshua on his own. The boy proved to be a remarkable student. He already had begun to teach himself Hebrew with a Hebrew-Spanish dictionary, and he quickly learned the prayers and rituals followed by Sephardic Jews. Like his father, Joshua became a leader and teacher, instructing followers in Lima, Trujillo, and Cajamarca.

In 1980, Villanueva paid his first visit to the Israeli embassy, seeking support for his congregation's desire to be accepted as Jews. Officials there greeted him warmly and helped introduce him to Israeli businessmen who were visiting Peru. The officials also told Villanueva about a national Bible contest they were sponsoring.

The embassy eventually received more than 300 entries for the contest from throughout Peru. Most of them came from the Colegio León Pinelo, the private Jewish school in Lima. There was one contestant from Trujillo, a young man named Víctor Chico, who was a member of Villanueva's congregation. His only training was that he had studied and worshiped with Segundo and Álvaro Villanueva and had closely read the books Rabbi Hamu had loaned them.

The results of the contest were announced that spring, and they stunned the Lima Jewish community. The winner was Víctor Chico, who was not even considered Jewish. One of Villanueva's followers would represent Peru in the international Bible contest in Jerusalem.

The Israeli government paid all of Chico's expenses and provided him and the other contestants with tours of the ancient Jewish sites he had read about, including the remaining wall of the Second Temple, which was expanded by Herod. He visited the tombs of Jewish sages, the fortress at Masada where Jewish patriots held out against the Romans, and the farm communes in the countryside. Chico was astonished by how easy it was to be Jewish in Israel. Kosher meat was available in all the markets; nearly all the restaurants were kosher. There were synagogues and religious schools everywhere; Orthodox Jews with side curls and black hats walked the streets among Israeli soldiers in uniform and businesspeople in suits. To Chico, the Jewish homeland was a blend of ancient majesty and modern conveniences.

When he returned to Peru, Chico brought the congregation the *Shulchan Aruch,* the code of Jewish law first published in the sixteenth century. A teacher from the Jewish school translated it into Spanish for them. Chico returned also with recordings of Israeli songs and with tales of the Holy Land. Perhaps, Villanueva thought, this country where people were proud to be Jews could be their homeland as well. If the 300 members of the congregation could convert to Judaism and move to Israel, they could worship freely as Jews and their children could marry Jews.

Villanueva shared his thoughts with his young disciple. But Chico told him flatly that emigration to Israel wasn't feasible. It might be realistic for them to emigrate to the United States and practice as Jews there, he said, but to be accepted as Jews in Israel would require more than Rabbi Hamu's help. They would need an Orthodox conversion, almost unheard of in South America.

Chico knew that Orthodox Jews had long been opposed to encouraging conversion; group conversion to Judaism was virtually unprecedented, at least in modern times. The last recorded mass conversion, of the pagan Idumeans and Galileans in ancient Israel, took place in the second century B.C.E. Even if conversion was possible, most of the congregants were too poor to pay for the airfare to Israel and settlement costs. So in addition to help from Orthodox rabbis, they would need assistance from the Israeli government. It was one thing for the members of the group to imitate the practices of Jews and follow their laws, Chico told Villanueva, but to actually become Jews and settle in Israel would require something close to a miracle. Villanueva wasn't dissuaded; he had ceaselessly believed in the impossible.

JEWS HAVE NOT always been opposed to reaching out to non-Jews. During the biblical period, the Hebrew kingdom expanded through intermarriage and conquest. But when the Jews returned to ancient Israel 2,500 years ago, after their exile in Babylonia, their leaders prohibited intermarriage in an effort to preserve the religion. The Book of Ruth, in which the non-Jew Ruth marries a Jew and is accepted as Jewish, is thought to have been written in protest of those decrees.

In exile, Jewish leaders tried to protect the faith from assimilation. When the Jews returned to power in ancient Israel, however, they welcomed—and sometimes compelled—conversion. During the Hasmonean dynasty 2,100 years ago, as they conquered other territories and peoples, Jews often forced their new subjects to convert or be killed. They also became active proselytizers among the Greeks. Proselytizing continued after the destruction of the Second Temple and under Roman rule. Scholars suggest that conversion was responsible for much of the rapid growth of the Jewish population in central Asia, Arabia, North Africa, and the Middle East. Some historians estimate that conversions, particularly among slaves, helped double the number of Jews between the seventh and eighth centuries. Judaism was no longer defined by race, ancestry, or territory. It was open to anyone who followed its beliefs and practices.

The dramatic increase in the Jewish population led to hostility from Christian and Muslim rulers. In the Middle Ages, both religions banned Jewish proselytizing in the countries they controlled, motivating the Jews to turn inward and once again redefine themselves. Persecution and prejudice drove Jewish leaders to protect their identities, as they had done during the Babylonian exile, and to oppose what they feared would be a dilution of their faith. Judaism became an exclusive religion that did not seek converts, although many conversions—particularly in Russia—were performed into the eighteenth and nineteenth centuries. In modern times, Reform and Conservative rabbis have been willing to perform conversions for non-Jews who plan to marry Jews and raise their children as Jews, but most rabbis generally discourage potential converts.

AFTER CHICO'S RETURN from Israel, David Liss, an engineer from Rishon Le Zion, an Israeli town south of Tel

Aviv, contacted rabbinic officials in Israel on Villanueva's behalf. He had met Villanueva through the Israeli embassy in Lima. Liss urged the rabbis to provide training and assistance for Villanueva's congregation. After repeated inquiries, they eventually agreed to send a representative, Baruch Adler, to visit Villanueva and his followers in Peru. Rabbi Adler quizzed them extensively about their practices and how they observed the Sabbath and other holidays.

"He was very demanding of us," Villanueva recalls with disappointment. "He wasn't satisfied with our knowledge and said we still had much to learn."

Liss persisted and wrote to others he thought might be more receptive, including Haim Avni, a professor at Hebrew University in Jerusalem. "It would be a great *mitzvah* for Judaism if something is done for this group," Liss wrote. Avni thought he could help. He passed the letter on to a rabbi who had previously worked at the university. The rabbi's name was Eliyahu Avichail, widely known as the founder of Amishav (My People Return), an organization dedicated to finding lost and dispersed Jews and returning the Ten Lost Tribes to Israel. The letter from Liss intrigued Rabbi Avichail. He had handled a similar request a few years earlier.

In 1984, the head of a small group from the southeastern coast of Mexico had visited Avichail in Jerusalem. The man said he represented about 300 people in Jalapa and Veracruz, less than 200 miles from Mexico City. They followed practices spelled out in the Hebrew Bible, including dietary laws; worshiped on the Sabbath and Jewish holidays; and had built their own synagogue. Mexican rabbis had refused to convert them. The group appealed to the chief rabbi of Israel, who recommended they meet with Avichail. In 1985, Avichail traveled to Mexico, questioned members of the community, and helped convert about 100 of them. Most of those who were converted later settled in Israel.

"Jewish law says that if you have people like this, people who have deep motivation to be Jews, you have to help them," Avichail said later.

The Peruvian community seemed eerily similar to the Mexican group. Both had come to Judaism on their own, through the pages of the Hebrew Bible. Avichail worried that he might be opening up the floodgates for thousands of new converts to Judaism.

Avichail recognized, however, that his work with the Mexicans and the Peruvians might generate support for his other work, his efforts to find the Lost Tribes of Israel and to discover Marranos who hoped to return to Judaism. The Peruvians also had strong backing from David Kiperstok, a Jew from Lima who had immigrated to Israel. In 1987, Kiperstok and his wife attended services with Villanueva's congregation in Peru. When he returned to Israel, Kiperstok conveyed his enthusiasm for the group to Avichail and brought him a videotape of the congregation. In addition, both Rabbi Hamu and Jacob Krauss, the Orthodox rabbi in Lima, offered their support. Perhaps most convincing was a letter in nearly flawless Hebrew from Villanueva's son, Joshua.

In the summer of 1988, Avichail sent Jonathan Segal to Peru

to investigate. Segal was an anthropology student and engineer who had traveled with Avichail in search of Lost Tribes in India and Afghanistan. In Peru, Segal interviewed Villanueva and members of his congregation about their knowledge of Judaism. He was far more optimistic about the congregation than Rabbi Adler had been five years earlier.

Segal returned to Israel to tell Avichail he was convinced of their sincerity. He reported that Villanueva had made, from leather and cedar wood, his own *tefillin*, the black leather cubes that contain four sections of the Torah written on parchment, which observant Jewish men strap to their arms and foreheads. Each weekday morning as he began his daily prayers, Villanueva wrapped one set of straps around his left hand and arm, with one cube facing his heart, and placed another cube in the center of his forehead. He completed his prayers and, since the congregation had only one pair, passed the *tefillin* among the other adult male members so they could pray. Villanueva also had borrowed a *chummash*, a book containing the Hebrew text of the Five Books of Moses as it appears in the Torah. Villanueva copied the pages onto cloth and sewed them into a long scroll bound by wooden handles, reproducing a Torah much like those kept in the arks of Jewish synagogues. The congregation, which now called itself B'nai Moshe (Children of Moses), even had begun to build its own synagogue, Segal said.

Segal also conveyed his support for the Peruvians to leaders of the Lubavitch movement to which he belonged. The Lubavitch sect had been founded about 1800 when Rabbi Schneur Zalman established a court in what is now Belarus. Schneur

Zalman was a brilliant scholar and follower of Hasidism, the eighteenth-century movement that embraced mysticism and spirituality. The Hasids transformed Judaism into a religion that appealed to alienated Jewish peasants throughout Eastern Europe. In 1820, Schneur Zalman's son and successor moved his court to Lubavitch, a small Belarussian town. Since that time, its followers have been known as Lubavitchers.

In 1940, Yosef Yitzhak, the sixth Lubavitcher rabbi, immigrated to the United States and settled in Brooklyn. Most of his followers later joined him. He appointed his son-in-law, Menachem (Mendel) Schneerson, to head a network of organizations known as Habad, the original name for their sect and a Hebrew acronym for wisdom, understanding, and knowledge. Habad established a publishing house, which spread information about Judaism, and a social welfare network to assist the poor. Yosef Yitzhak's decision to escape Europe, in addition to his son-in-law's outreach, transformed what had been a small, contained movement. When nearly all of European Jewry and their rabbis were murdered in the Holocaust, the Lubavitchers who survived in Brooklyn became a prominent force in Orthodox Judaism.

Menachem Schneerson was elected leader of the movement in 1950 after his father-in-law's death. The new rebbe rapidly expanded Habad, founding a women's organization, a youth movement, Jewish schools, summer camps, and Habad houses in Europe, Asia, Latin America, and the Soviet Union. Their publishing house became the largest distributor of Jewish books in the world. In the United States, Lubavitchers used billboards and mobile vans called *"mitzvah* tanks" to advertise their movement, circulate photographs of Schneerson, and spread the word that the Messiah was coming.

The Lubavitchers do not promote conversion, yet they encourage Jews to follow Orthodox practices. Under Menachem Schneerson's leadership, their evangelism took on a messianic fervor, reflecting the rebbe's message that the apocalypse was imminent. The rebbe often spoke of events in the Middle East and Russia as signs of the Messiah's impending arrival; his words were taped and broadcast throughout the world by satellite and on the Internet. Some of his followers began to suggest that the rebbe, who had no children and had not named a successor, was himself the Messiah.

Shortly after Segal's visit in 1988, the Lubavitchers sent Myron Zuber, a retired chemist from Monsey, New York, to visit with Villanueva. Zuber, a portly, avuncular man, helped bring the story of B'nai Moshe to a wider audience, including members of Kulanu, the group that had assisted the Abayudaya in Uganda.

Zuber's account of his visit, published in the Kulanu newsletter, was headlined "Converting Inca Indians in Peru." It recounted the history of the congregation, beginning with what Zuber called Villanueva's "religious transformation" in Trujillo in 1966. Villanueva, according to Zuber, was excommunicated from the Catholic church for embracing Judaism, and ostracized from his community. Then, Zuber wrote, Villanueva went to Spain for six months to learn about Judaism from the community in Madrid and to study the works of two great Spanish-born Jewish scholars, Moses Maimonides from the twelfth century and Don Isaac Abravanel from the fifteenth. He returned to Peru and soon attracted 500 followers. The Jews in Lima rejected Villanueva and his congregation, Zuber wrote, because Incas were viewed as inferior.

Zuber's published account continues:

In 1985, [Villanueva] contacted the Lubavitcher Rebbe and Lubavitch Rabbi Chadokov (his secretary) immediately got in touch with me since he said I was "proficient in the laws of ritual slaughter [he had taken a course at a local community college] and adept at mingling with people." I agreed to travel to Peru and aid these Inca Indians in their quest to become Jewish and immediately enrolled in Spanish studies. I arrived in Peru in 1988 and discovered that the people were genuinely committed.

Zuber said he instructed members of the congregation in how to observe the Sabbath and keep kosher, introduced them to Jewish songs and dances, and, at their insistence, taught them about reincarnation and the Messiah. He said he made many trips to the communities in Lima, Cajamarca, and Trujillo.

Nearly everything in Zuber's account varies considerably from the one told to me by Villanueva, including the suggestion that the members of B'nai Moshe were Incas. Some of them did have Indian ancestors, but none of them called himself an Inca. Zuber may have been drawn to the Peruvians because of mystical links between the Americas and the Jews dating back to biblical times. In the seventeenth century, Menashe ben Israel, a Dutch rabbi, wrote that descendants of the Ten Lost Tribes of Israel had settled in Latin America. He based his story on questionable reports from a Dutch Marrano sailor, who said he had discovered a group of Indians following Jewish rituals, including the recitation of the Hebrew prayer *Shema Yisrael* (Hear, O Israel). A French traveler later revived the legend linking Indians to the ancient Hebrews. In 1869, Onffroy de Thorón claimed that King Solomon's ships had reached the Amazon river basin and that many words in Quechua, the language of Andean natives, were similar to Hebrew.

Many other details—Villanueva says he began his studies in 1939, not 1966, in Cajamarca, not Trujillo; that he was neither ostracized nor excommunicated by the church; and that he had never been to Spain—also were changed in Zuber's retelling. Villanueva says Zuber played only a minor role in training the community; they had been observing the Sabbath for more than forty years and were well versed in Jewish laws and rituals long before Zuber arrived.

Some of the inconsistencies can be attributed to Zuber's limited knowledge of Spanish; he had studied the language at a community college for only a few months before he went to Peru. The remaining discrepancies are perhaps attributable to a Lubavitch tendency to take credit for remarkable events, including the victory of the Israeli army in the 1967 war, the freedoms achieved by Soviet Jews during *glasnost,* the support for Judaism and Israel by several American presidents, and the spiritual revival of Jewry worldwide, which, the Lubavitchers claim, will bring the coming of the Messiah.

Despite Zuber's inaccurate account, Villanueva's group now had the backing of both an influential Israeli rabbi, Eliyahu Avichail, and the powerful Lubavitchers. Villanueva's improbable quest seemed to be possible. With the support of the Israeli chief rabbi, Avichail made plans to organize a rabbinic court to go to Peru to officially examine members of the congregation and convert those who were deserving. In August 1989, Rabbi Avichail and Rabbi Mordechai Oriah, head of the religious court in Haifa, flew to Peru, where they joined Rabbi Krauss from Lima and convened a *bet din*, a rabbinic court, to convert members of B'nai Moshe to Judaism.

SCHOLARLY ACCOUNTS DIFFER over when formal rituals for conversion to Judaism first took place. Some see Ruth's pledge to Naomi—"Where you go, I will go, and where you lodge, I will lodge; your people shall be my people, and your God my God; where you die, I will die and there I will be buried" (Ruth 1:16)—as an ancient formula for becoming a Jew. The story of Ruth is set in the eleventh century B.C.E.

The legal rules for conversion emerged slowly. By the second century C.E., the requirements included circumcision for males, immersion, and sacrifice. While the Temple stood, potential converts were expected to offer birds or cattle for sacrifice, and the blood of the offering was sprinkled on the Temple altar. All sacrifices were eliminated after the Temple was destroyed; they may have been replaced for a time by a requirement that converts set aside funds for rebuilding it. There was a great deal of dispute over which rituals were required. Female converts were to be immersed in pure water; the commentaries differ over whether males needed both circumcision and immersion. Some sages required a male convert to undergo *atafat dam*—in which at least a drop of blood is drawn from the penis—to become a Jew; others wrote that the ritual is not required for a male who already is circumcised. When blood was taken, the rabbis recited a benediction:

> Blessed are You, our God, King of the Universe, who has sanctified us with Your commandments and has commanded us to circumcise converts and to cause the drops of blood of the covenant to flow from them, because if it were not for the blood of the covenant, heaven and earth would not endure, as it is said: "If not My covenant by day and by night, I would not have appointed ordinances of heaven and earth." Blessed are You, God, who makes the covenant.

Unlike the benediction for males born to a Jewish mother, the benediction for converts includes no specific reference to the covenant of Abraham because ancient commentaries suggest that converts make up a different category of Jews. Converts are, however, called sons or daughters of Abraham and Sarah as part of their Hebrew names.

Early in the second century C.E., as Emperor Hadrian persecuted the rebellious Jews and issued his edicts banning proselytizing, the rabbis established a procedure for interrogating potential converts:

> If at the present time a man desires to become a proselyte, he is to be addressed as follows. "What reason have you for desiring to become a proselyte; do you not know that Israel at the present time are [sic] persecuted and oppressed, de-

spised, harassed, and overcome by afflictions?" If he replies,
"I know and yet am unworthy," he is accepted forthwith, and
is given instruction in some of the minor and some of the
major commandments.

The passage seems to substantiate arguments that non-Jews
were not initially required to undergo extensive training until
after they had been converted.

In modern times, potential converts are expected to be well
versed in Judaism before conversion. Most rabbis require immersion for all converts, and circumcision for males. They also
require a *bet din* to question the candidate's motives for conversion and his or her knowledge of Jewish law.

ON AUGUST 24, 1989, rabbis Avichail and Oriah arrived in Trujillo, where they met Rabbi Krauss and members of
Villanueva's congregation. The rabbis questioned them intensively about their knowledge of Judaism and whether they lived
Jewish lives. After three days, the three rabbis selected eight
families, totaling about sixty people, for conversion.

"The questions were easy for us," Villanueva recalls. "We
had been following these practices for years. We had been reading the Book."

The rabbis decided not to convert unmarried people or anyone who would not commit to settling in Israel.

"The core of conversion is that someone believes in Judaism
and wants to fulfill the *mitzvot* [Jewish laws]," Avichail told *The
Jerusalem Post* a few months later. "A convert has to undertake

to fulfill the commandments. There would be no reason to convert these people if they were going to stay in Peru, because under the conditions there, even if they would not assimilate, their children would. They could not live as Torah-true Jews there."

The rabbis then determined which of the potential male converts already had ritual circumcisions. They approved those whom Dr. Kogan, a Jew, had circumcised, but required *atafat dam* for the five young people who had been circumcised by a non-Jewish doctor.

Then the three rabbis and sixty potential converts drove by car and bus to the Moche river, nine miles outside of Trujillo, which was named for a tribal civilization that predated the Incas. The converts sang Hebrew folk songs during the bus ride. At the banks of the river, the women gathered behind a stand of trees, took off their clothes, and donned white shrouds. In the cold wind that blew down from the Andes mountains, Rabbi Oriah's wife led them to the river in three groups, first the older women, then the girls, and finally the women with infants.

"They seemed like angels, coming from behind the trees in their shrouds," Rabbi Avichail tells me ten years later.

Each woman immersed herself three times and then repeated the prayers the rabbis recited. After the women finished, the men removed their clothes and stepped into the river to repeat the three immersions and prayers. When the ceremony was over, the three rabbis celebrated by rolling up their pant legs, jumping into the river, and reciting a blessing for the occasion.

The families then returned to Trujillo. In Villanueva's new synagogue, the rabbis performed brief marriage ceremonies for each of the married couples, sanctifying their marriages under Jewish law. The rabbis also filled out certificates officially recognizing the conversions and the marriages. The day ended with an evening of food, song, and dance.

Several days later, the *bet din* traveled to Lima, where they performed similar examinations, immersions, circumcisions, and marriages. About fifteen people from three families, including the Álvaro Villanueva family, passed the test. The immersions were performed in the choppy surf of the Pacific Ocean outside of Lima.

Fifty years after Segundo Villanueva first began reading his father's Bible and felt a powerful connection to the Jewish people, his family and some of his followers had officially become Jews. Now he would lead them to the Promised Land.

A few weeks after the ceremonies, Villanueva received a letter from the leaders of the Jewish community in Eilon Moreh, the home that Avichail had chosen for them in Israel. Fifteen families of religious nationalists had established the town ten years earlier in the hills overlooking Nablus, the farthest settlement into hostile Arab territory. It was not far from the site where, according to the Bible, God promised Abraham the Land of Israel and where Joseph is buried. The letter described the community, making clear that the settlement was near the center of the Intifada and at the forefront of a highly charged political and religious debate.

Avichail's mission clearly had a political component. The religious nationalist movement, which was committed to expanding settlements in the occupied West Bank as a means of hastening the arrival of the Messiah, inspired and supported much of Avichail's work. In the 1970s, the radical nationalists had established settlements throughout the heart of Arab-occupied territory in the West Bank. In 1980, they started building towns in the hills near Nablus, the largest Arab city in the West Bank and the center of Palestinian opposition to Israel.

The settlers eventually won approval from the Israeli government, which was controlled by the Likud party, with support from the religious right. The government offered generous subsidies for settlers and businesses that relocated to the West Bank. As Arab unrest spread through the territories, however, the pace of settlement slowed and Israelis became increasingly reluctant to move there. The new settlers were mostly immigrants, including refugees from the Soviet Union and ultra-Orthodox Jews from the United States. Most of them lived in constant danger of reprisals by Arab militants and were less well off than the average Israeli immigrant. Critics said the settlers were being used as human shields against the next wave of Arab attacks and as pawns to serve the religious nationalists' goal of incorporating the territories into the State of Israel. But Villanueva and his followers were eager to go.

In February 1990, six months after the conversions, the Jewish Agency notified Villanueva that all of the converts were to come to Israel immediately. The Israeli government had made the airline reservations and paid for the tickets. The notice came with almost no warning, and the converts had no time to sell their homes or goods. They flew on El Al to Tel Aviv, where they took a bus to Eilon Moreh, arriving at 2:00 A.M. About 100 residents, many of them Russian immigrants, greeted them with Hebrew songs and Israeli dances. To Villanueva, the hills of Samaria looked like miniature versions of the mountains near Cajamarca, where he was born.

For six months, Villanueva and his followers lived in mobile homes while they studied Hebrew and an Uruguayan-born rabbi instructed them further in Jewish law. They received monthly allowances from the government. By the beginning of the Jewish New Year that fall, nearly all of the young men had found jobs as farmers and laborers, the children were enrolled in a religious school, and all of the families had been provided with new homes and furniture.

Two years after the first conversions, in August 1991, another *bet din* came to Peru and converted nearly 100 more members of B'nai Moshe. Myron Zuber, the Lubavitcher from Monsey, returned to Peru to participate in the ceremony. Among the converts was Margalit, a teacher from Lima in her late thirties, whom Zuber had met on his earlier visit. After her conversion, Zuber, then seventy years old and a recent widower, married her and brought her with him to the United States, where she gave birth to a son several years later. Over the next two years, the remaining converts joined Villanueva and the other settlers in Eilon Moreh and Kfar Tapuach.

TEN YEARS AFTER two groups of Villanueva's followers have converted and settled in Israel, a remnant is left behind in Trujillo, worshiping in the synagogue Villanueva helped build. I join them for services on a cloudy August day. A few drops of rain, quite rare on the dry coastal plain of Trujillo, sprinkle through the flat thatched roof of the synagogue. The bare lightbulbs overhead glare brightly off the whitewashed brick walls. I sit in the sanctuary with the men and boys, on small wooden and straw chairs. Hebrew names are engraved on the backs of some of the chairs—Yishay, Nachshon, Yehudah. On one side, a long blue shower curtain separates us from the women's section; on the other side, a partition of woven hemp divides the sanctuary from the dining room. A small wooden box on a table serves as an ark. It holds a miniature version of the Torah, donated by Kulanu, made of paper instead of parch-ment and normally used to train students.

The synagogue is on the outskirts of the city, in a district called Esperanza, or Hope. The congregation now calls itself B'nai Avraham, the phrase that identifies converts to Judaism. The members dream of formally converting and joining the other Peruvians in Israel, where they can raise their children among Jews. Most of them have some family members in Eilon Moreh who have been urging the rabbis in Jerusalem to send a third *bet din* to Peru. The rabbis' response has not been en-couraging; the push to import settlers for the occupied territo-ries has slowed.

In the kitchen behind us, with separate sinks, counters, and utensils for milk and meat, several of the women spoon out a Sabbath lunch of pasta and fish, cooked the day before and kept warm overnight in large metal pots wrapped in cloth. As we sing the final verses of the afternoon service, the women emerge from the kitchen and place the food on the tables in the din-ing room. Each table is covered with a freshly ironed tablecloth on which is placed a vase of red, yellow, and purple roses; a *chal-*

lah covered with an embroidered blue-and-white cloth cover; and a decanter of dark red homemade wine.

Thirty men, women, and children from five families—Raza, Luján, Vásquez, Mendoza, and Pérez—soon gather around the tables. Some of the women are dressed in dark, fitted suits and felt bowler hats, gifts from Myron Zuber. Most of the men wear hand-knitted skullcaps, white shirts, and suit jackets; several have *tzitzim*—fringes from undergarments worn by Orthodox males—dangling alongside their trousers. One older man wears a bright yellow New York Yankees baseball cap.

Two days earlier, Rosa Valderrama, Próspero Luján, and I helped Yishay Raza, the president of the congregation, prepare his late wife's gravestone in the St. John the Baptist cemetery. Yishay invites me to join him at his family's table along with his daughter, Raquel; son, Menachem; Menachem's wife, Rivka; and their infant son, Baruch. Raquel has taken over her mother's duties and brings the food to our table. Menachem balances Baruch on his lap as he pours each of us a brimming glass of wine. Then Yishay, in halting Hebrew, leads the prayers over the wine and *challah*. The wine tastes like unsweetened grape juice; the *challah*, made with dark flour, is soft and chewy.

I can hear the sounds of another congregation singing not far away. Yishay says they are members of Israel de Dios, the group that Villanueva founded in Cajamarca two generations earlier. This group still follows the practices Villanueva preached in his early years, copying the rituals of the ancient Hebrews as spelled out in the Bible. There are thousands of them in congregations in Trujillo, Cajamarca, and other towns in northern Peru. As the sounds of Hebrew prayer from B'nai Avraham meld with the

Spanish psalms sung by members of Israel de Dios, I wonder whether this small remnant from the synagogue in Trujillo will be able to join the others in Israel or whether they will lose hope and disappear. Will the Peruvians in the West Bank soon assimilate into Israeli society? Will their grandchildren know the story of how they became Jews? Perhaps in a generation or two, all that will remain of Villanueva's legacy in Peru is a handful of Hebrew gravestones and Israel de Dios, the congregation he founded on his journey toward Judaism.

In the 1960s, the Peruvian government . . . isolation of the jungle. James D. Rudolph, *Peru: The Evolution of a Crisis* (Westport, CT: Praeger, 1992), pp. 48–49, 63–64; William P. Mitchell, *Peasants on the Edge* (Austin, TX: 1991 University of Texas Press,), pp. 164–66.

Perhaps the strangest of these sects . . . Associated Press Worldstream, September 9, 1995; UPI, August 28 and 30, 1995.

European Jews, including industrialists . . . Ninetyfive percent of Lima's Jewish children attended it. Judith Laikin Elkin, *Jews of the Latin American Republics* (Chapel Hill: University of North Carolina Press, 1980), pp. 46–47, 65–66, 176.

Jews have not always been opposed to reaching out . . . In the Middle Ages, both religions banned Jewish proselytizing . . . Joseph K. Rosenbloom, *Conversion to Judaism* (Cincinnati: Hebrew Union College Press, 1978), pp. 15–46.

"It would be a great *mitzvah* . . ." Rabbi Eliyahu Avichail, *The Tribes of Israel* (Jerusalem: Amishav, 1989), p. 175.

The Lubavitch sect had been founded . . . Some of his followers began to suggest that the rebbe . . . was himself the Messiah. Michael Specter, "The Oracle of Crown Heights," *New York Times Magazine*, March 15, 1992; Allan Nadler, "Despite All Odds: The Story of Lubavitch," book review, *New Republic,* May 4, 1992; Alexander Zvielli and Herb Keinon, "Menachem Schneerson, Leader of Habad," *Jerusalem Post,* June 13, 1994.

Zuber's account of his visit . . .   Kulanu newsletter <http://www.ubalt.edu/www/kulanu/zuber.html> and <http://www.ubalt.edu/Kulanu/peru.html>.

A French traveler later revived . . .   Ariel Segal, *Jews of the Amazon* (Philadelphia: Jewish Publication Society, 1999), p. 23.

. . . Lubavitch tendency to take credit for remarkable events . . . Nadler, "Despite All Odds."

In August 1989, Rabbi Avichail and Rabbi Mordechai Oriah . . . Avichail, *The Tribes of Israel;* Herb Keinon, "Extraordinary New Jews," *Jerusalem Post,* March 9, 1990.

Scholarly accounts differ . . . commentaries differ over whether males needed both circumcision and immersion.   Robert M. Seltzer, "Joining the Jewish People from Biblical to Modern Times," in *Pushing the Faith,* Martin E. Marty and Frederick E. Greenspan, eds. (New York: Crossroad; 1988), pp. 41–53; Gary C. Porton, *The Stranger Within Your Gates* (Chicago: University of Chicago Press, 1994), pp. 132–54.

"Blessed are You, our God . . ."   Porton, *The Stranger Within Your Gates,* p. 140.

"If at the present time . . ."   Seltzer, "Joining the Jewish People," p. 51.

Fifteen families of religious nationalists . . .   Herb Keinon, "Amazon Jungle Community May Come; More Peruvian Olim Arrive in Eilon Moreh," *Jerusalem Post,* August 16, 1991; Keinon, "Extraordinary New Jews."

In the 1970s, the radical nationalists . . .   Jeff Black, "Root Causes." *Jerusalem Post,* December 20, 1991; Abraham Rabinovich, "Katzover: Determined but Biding His Time," *Jerusalem Post,* December 29, 1995.

The settlers eventually won approval . . .   Don Peretz, *The West Bank: History, Politics, Society, and Economics* (London: Westview Press, 1986), pp. 49–54; Efraim Ben-Zadok, ed., *Local Communities and the Israeli Polity* (Albany: State University Press of New York, 1993), pp. 48–49.

Chapter Three

CHILDREN OF MANASSEH

Jeremiah Hnamte carefully lifts the simple white cloth with Hebrew lettering. Beneath it is a platter stacked with *chapatis*, the round, flat bread that is standard fare in India. Yet these *chapatis* are different, crisp and somewhat brittle. Other women in town might have mocked Jeremiah's wife, Chhuandi, had they seen her fry them on her gas stove a few hours earlier. She purposefully used low heat to prevent them from rising.

On another plate in front of Jeremiah, she has arranged a roasted chicken leg, some sprigs of a bitter leaf called *bakkhate*, bowls of boiled eggs and salt water, some lettuce, and a mixture of nuts, apples, wine, and coconut. Next to it is a pitcher of grape juice, a dozen glasses, and a white ceramic cup inscribed with blue Hebrew letters.

It is now sundown in Mizoram, but a brilliant white light shines through the small window above the kitchen and floods the surrounding hills and gorges where the mango and papaya trees are bearing their first fruits. It is the glow of the first full moon of spring. Under a similar glow more than three millennia earlier, Moses led his people out of the land of Egypt. Forty years later, on Mt. Sinai, God commanded Moses and the Jewish people to celebrate the exodus with the Festival of Passover, beginning on the first full moon of the Jewish month of Nisan, and to commemorate their hurried escape by eating unleavened bread.

Here in this remote corner of northeastern India, nearly 4,000 miles to the east of Sinai and far from the Jewish mainstream, Jeremiah Hnamte, his friends, and his family are seated around the table, reliving this deliverance from bondage. They, too, hope to find their freedom in the land of Israel.

Jeremiah recites the words—"This is the bread of affliction which our ancestors ate in the land of Egypt"—from the newly printed pamphlet in front of him, titled *"Haggada shel Pessach."* It is a Passover prayer book in which the Hebrew has been transliterated to look like Mizo, the local dialect.

Jeremiah, a stocky, almost cherubic man with brown skin, high cheekbones, and almond-shaped eyes, sets the plate of *chapati*s back on the table, and Chhuandi, sitting across from him in her brocaded white blouse, blue felt hat, and pleated purple skirt, leads the guests in singing the familiar opening verse of the Four Questions. The words take on an Oriental inflection as they sing in Hebrew, "Why is this night different from all other nights?" The singing is nearly drowned out by the screams of a nine-month-old girl in her father's lap, who quiets down when her mother scoops her up and wraps her in a long white cloth with black stripes that bears a strong resemblance to a Jewish prayer shawl.

In Mizoram and neighboring Manipur, hilly, sparsely populated Indian provinces wedged between Bangladesh and Burma, a people known as the Mizos are embracing Judaism. Many of them believe they are descended from one of the biblical Lost Tribes of Israel, although there is little evidence of their origins other than folktales. Mizo legends and songs suggest that thousands of years ago, their ancestors migrated east from ancient Israel and eventually settled in China. More than 300 years ago, they moved west and established tribal villages in Burma, Mizoram, and Manipur. Yet their past still called to them. In the 1950s, some villagers proclaimed they heard mystical voices linking their people to the Hebrews of the Bible. Others joined them in their efforts to follow Jewish practices and to move to Israel, which they consider their ancient homeland. With the assistance of the same rabbi who championed the Peruvian peasants, more than 300 settled in the West Bank and the Gaza Strip in recent years and formally converted to Judaism. Thousands more, including Jeremiah and his family, hope to follow.

THE MIZOS—ALSO known as Chins or Kukis—were fierce warriors who fought rival tribes and foreign invaders in and around steep gorges and bamboo forests. Each village, usually located on the crest of a ridge, existed as a separate state, ruled by a hereditary chief and a council of elders. The villagers followed a code of conduct that required them to be unselfish and considerate. The chief and elders issued fines for theft, assault, and other violations of their customs and morals. There was no written language; the rules were part of their oral tradition. Their religious beliefs had little in common with the predominant religions in China, from where they had originally come, or with the religions in Burma and India.

The Mizos believed that evil spirits lived in the mountains, trees, springs, and rocks, and that the spirits would punish with illness or death anyone who passed them. To placate the spirits, a village priest performed animal sacrifices on a small bamboo altar. Parents often gave their children unpleasant names so the spirits would find them unattractive. (Mizos customarily have only one name; some of those who practice Judaism, like Jeremiah, have added Hebrew first names.) Another, higher-ranking priest performed ceremonies and sacrifices for the entire village.

The Mizos believed in one high God, a kind and powerful being often called Pathian, who created the world. They celebrated three annual festivals, one in December at the end of the harvest, one in the spring after a new hillside had been cleared for planting, and one in September, the season of the first fruits, which honored the dead. During the first two feasts, the high priest sacrificed a pig and other domestic animals, and villagers celebrated by dancing and drinking large quantities of rice beer. For the mourning festival, Mizos set out food for their dead relatives. They also believed in an afterlife. Those who had hunted large animals or sponsored a series of feasts for the village would enter paradise, where everything was luxurious and abundant. Others would enter the village of the dead, a shadowy underworld.

Mizoram, which means Land of the Hill People, is roughly the size of the state of Maine and was among the last areas of Southeast Asia to fall under British control, in the 1890s. Mizos continued to raid British tea plantations into the 1920s, yet British missionaries had remarkable success among them. The missionaries claimed to find similarities between Western religions and Mizo tribal rituals and customs; they built churches on the sites of village sacrificial altars and taught the Mizos biblical passages about ancient Hebrew priests, sacrifices, and festivals. By the 1980s, nearly 85 percent of the people in Mizoram and 30 percent in Manipur had converted to Christianity.

The Welsh Presbyterian evangelists who had come to the region to spread Christianity also inspired the emergence of revivalist sects, which focused on the Holy Spirit, prophecy, and speaking in tongues. Although the Presbyterian church later discouraged such practices, they could not suppress them. The Mizos, who had felt restrained by conventional Christianity, celebrated Christ with dances and tribal music in their evangelical churches. They also returned to beliefs in the supernatural.

In 1925, one Mizo named Chaltuahkhuma, after comparing Mizo beliefs with passages in the Bible, concluded that his people might be a Lost Tribe of Israel. A Mizo revivalist repeated the assertion several years later, claiming that the Mizos descended from the Tribe of Manasseh. He noted that many Mizo prayers, passed down by the elders, had invoked the name of Manasseh, whom the Bible names as the elder of Joseph's two sons.

The resurgence of the myth took hold in the 1950s, when two farmers from a small village in Mizoram claimed they had heard and seen visions from a Holy Spirit who told them they had descended from the Lost Tribes. Darnghaka and Chala, two members of a United Pentecostal church in the village of Buallawn, preached about visions they had received and announced that the Mizos were destined to return to Israel. Doliana, a humble man in his late seventies who lives in a simple wooden hut several miles down the hill from Jeremiah's home, remembers those visions vividly. He was a member of that church and served as Chala's secretary.

"Those of us in the United Pentecostal church always had loved Israel, we always had wanted to know how we could become Israelites," recalls Doliana, a thin, wiry man whose taut, lined features brighten as he talks about his days with Chala. "The elders had told us about the rituals from our past, and we knew that Hebrew and Mizo cultures were very much alike."

Like the Hebrews, Mizos believed in one God, the creator of all things, and did not worship idols. They offered sacrifices through their priests, as the ancient Hebrews had done, and the dates of two of their holidays approximated the Hebrew calendar for Passover and Sukkot. Mizo women wore a shawl that looked much like a Jewish prayer shawl, and buried their husbands in it.

Doliana says:

In 1955, Darnghaka and Chala began to have visions. They were like movies in their minds; they would lie down in trances at their homes at night. The Holy Spirit told Darnghaka that we were Israel people and we had to go there. Chala said God had told him He wanted to make Mizoram Israel, that Mizoram was part of the same fruit as Israel. We cried for Israel—everyone wanted to go.

Each Sunday they would come to church and speak from the pulpit, telling us about their visions and how we would move to Israel. The news spread all over Mizoram. We were so happy. We danced, played drums, and sang spiritual songs.

The memory inspires Doliana to put down his cup of red tea, clear his throat, and sing one of those songs:

When I reach that beautiful city,
I will long no more for this desert land.
Oh, I will rest on the holy mountain in Israel.

Doliana continues:

One night the Spirit told Darnghaka he would find a message on the right side of a newspaper from northeast India that wrote about Israel. Two members of our congregation flew to Imphal [now the capital of the neighboring province of Manipur, northeast of Mizoram] to look for the newspaper, but they couldn't find it. Then they went to Silchar [in

Assam province, northwest of Mizoram] and found a copy of *The Middle East Observer.* They saw an article on the right side of the front page that said the Israeli government was building many houses for people to come to Israel.

They returned home and wrote a letter in English to [Israeli prime minister] Ben Gurion, which the editor of *The Observer* forwarded to him. The letter said that Israel people were living here, that we were very poor and eager to come to Israel. It also said that Jerusalem had fallen to foreigners twice before but would not be conquered again. Ben Gurion forwarded the letter to the Knesset [Israeli Parliament], and they replied to us. They said that they were very happy to hear from us but wanted to know why we were certain that Jerusalem would not fall again. Darnghaka replied that we had been told this by the Holy Spirit.

The Israeli officials told the Mizos that they could not help them get to Israel right away but suggested they contact the Israeli consul in Calcutta. Three members of the church flew there. He goes on:

The consul said he was so happy to meet us after we had been lost for two thousand years. He wrote down the names of the members of our church in a book—there were one hundred forty members, including many new ones who had joined us from other villages. The consul said he would send the names to Jerusalem. But he said there were many other people who wanted to live in Israel, and since we lived peacefully in India, we could wait.

After that, we studied the Bible and our history and

changed our services. We celebrated the Sabbath on Saturday and began to call our church a synagogue. The men and women sat separately. Darnghaka, Chala, and I preached, read the Bible, mostly the Old Testament, and led the congregation in songs. After lunch, we studied the Bible and talked about our nation and our origins.

We also celebrated the other holidays in the Bible. In September, we built huts outside the village and prayed inside them during Sukkot. Every April 14, we celebrated Passover, just as the Hebrew people did in the Bible. We had a feast inside the church, with a table for each family, and ate bitter herbs with rice. We ate hurriedly, as if we were about to flee from the Egyptians. Three priests—older, respected men from the village—killed a young goat on a stone altar in front of the church as a few other men watched, and the rest of the congregation sang and danced inside. The priests wore dark blue robes with ropes around their waists. They said prayers, cut the goat's neck, and collected the blood in a bowl. They spread the blood on the altar and on the door of the church. Then they went to every member's house and spread a daub of blood on each door with their hands. Later, we all ate the goat meat.

The congregation continued their new practices, based on passages in an English translation of the Hebrew Bible, for more than ten years. But they also did not stray far from what the missionaries had taught them. They worshiped Jesus and followed many other Christian practices. Like other Christian fundamentalists who interpret the Book of Revelations literally, they foresaw the war of Armageddon and believed that in Israel they would escape the destruction at the end of days. (The attraction to Israel remains common today among dozens of Christian evangelical sects in Mizoram.) What made the movement in Buallawn unusual was that Darnghaka and Chala's followers considered themselves descendants of the Lost Tribes and longed to settle in Israel before Armaggedon, during their own lifetimes.

The movement came to an abrupt end in 1966 when Indian troops battling Mizo rebels forced the villagers to leave Buallawn. The rebellion had begun in 1961, after famine and disease had devastated Mizoram. The famine seemed almost mystical. Every fifty years, the bamboo that covers the hillsides blooms with a brilliant yellow flower. The seeds from the flowers attract rats, which multiply rapidly after gorging on the seeds and then swarm over the villages, destroying rice crops and spreading cholera. The famine and cholera outbreak in 1959 killed thousands of Mizos; the Indian government did little to help.

The Mizos formed their own relief organization to provide food and health care. After the famine subsided, the organization spawned a guerrilla group, the Mizo National Front, which fought to secede from India. In 1966, rebels seized Aizawl, the capital of Mizoram. The Indian air force bombed and strafed the city, and tens of thousands of Indian troops invaded. The troops drove the rebels out of Aizawl and pursued them into the surrounding villages. To deny the rebels sanctuary, the army forced Mizos in the countryside to abandon their villages and then burned their homes and crops, a tactic American troops were using to fight the Viet Cong in nearby South Vietnam. The villagers were relocated into guarded settlements with strict curfews. Doliana remembers when the soldiers first came to Buallawn village.

One of the Indian colonels sent a messenger to get me in the fields one afternoon as I was harvesting rice. The messenger said the colonel had to meet with a representative of the Israel people before dark that day. I was afraid, shaking. I thought I was going to be punished. I went to a hut in the field to pray. But a voice in my heart told me not to be afraid, and my fear went away.

It was nearly dark by the time I got to Ratu, where the soldiers were encamped. There were hundreds of soldiers in the village. I reported to the colonel, as I had been instructed. The colonel seemed friendly. He asked me to explain why we called ourselves Israel people.

I told him our savior Jesus was of the Israel people and that we followed him. If Jesus was a Jew, we also are Jews.

The colonel asked me, "Who are your ancestors?" I said we descended from Joseph's son Manasseh and we had learned this from Darnghaka and Chala's visions, when the Holy Spirit came to us.

He asked me to write my name in his book and to drink zu [rice beer] with him. I said I didn't drink. [The missionaries had convinced most Mizos to stop drinking zu.] He didn't understand why we drank zu for the sacrament and not socially, but he gave me tea instead. He said he was glad I had come and that I should go home peacefully and not be afraid. He seemed upset that his messenger had frightened me. He sent me home with an escort of soldiers.

A few days later, the army resettled the villagers in Ratu and burned down all the houses and fields in Buallawn to prevent rebels from seeking out food and shelter there. The local officials in Ratu, convinced that those who called themselves Israel people supported the rebels, told them they could not continue their practices. Most rejoined the United Pentecostal church. One man from Buallawn eventually made it to Israel; another couple later joined Jeremiah Hnamte in a group that now practices Orthodox Judaism.

"Israel is still inside the heart of the people," Doliana says.

AS DARNGHAKA AND Chala's following in Buallawn waned during the military suppression in Mizoram, another group, also proclaiming Mizo links to the Lost Tribes, evolved independently in neighboring Manipur. This time, their contacts with the outside world moved them closer to Orthodox Judaism.

In Churachandpur, a small village about thirty-five miles from Imphal, the Reverend H. Thangruma, formerly a pastor affiliated with the United Pentecostal church, founded his own church. Thangruma had long believed, based on their ancient practices, that the Mizos were descendants of the Lost Tribes, either the Tribe of Ephraim or Manasseh. In 1964, he received some literature from the Zion Church of God in Jerusalem, a group of young people who were raised as Jews but profess a belief in Jesus. The way their teachings brought together traditions from both the Hebrew Bible and New Testament appealed to Thangruma. He founded his own Church of God based on those beliefs and established congregations in villages throughout Manipur and Mizoram. His was essentially a Christian church, though it differed from Christianity in that its members prayed and performed the sacrament on Saturdays and on the Jewish holidays of Passover, Shavuot, and Sukkot. And they didn't eat pork, a staple of the Mizo diet.

One member of the church in Churachandpur, a man named Thankamlova, soon began to doubt Thangruma's teachings. He sensed that the Church of God was an amalgamation, not a true religion. If Mizos were descendants of the Hebrews, Thankamlova reasoned, they should follow the Hebrew Bible more closely. Thankamlova left the church and, with a few friends, formed a small religious community that prayed in his home. They tried to carry out Hebrew practices described in the Bible, hoping to reconnect to what they believed were their ancient traditions.

"They prayed on Saturday, reading from the Bible and making it a holy day," says Joshua Benjamin, Thankamlova's grandson, who was an infant at the time. "They didn't cook on the Sabbath, so we had to eat cold food. They had a stone altar in Churachandpur, and I believe they performed sacrifices there. They celebrated the festivals in the Bible as well. But in the beginning, they couldn't leave Jesus Christ."

It was V. L. Benjamin—Thankamlova's son and Joshua's father—who led the community away from Christianity and introduced modern Jewish practices. He also helped spread

Judaism to other branches of the Church of God in Manipur and Mizoram.

"My father was a businessman who traded cloth," says Joshua, a diminutive, youthful-looking man who now lives in Israel's Gaza Strip with his wife and four children. "He traveled a lot. In the early seventies, he met some members of the Jewish community in Bombay."

There were actually two separate Jewish communities in Bombay, the B'nai Israel and the Baghdadis. The B'nai Israel, like the Mizos, claimed descent from the Ten Lost Tribes. They believed their ancestors were a small group of Jews shipwrecked off the west coast of India about 2,200 years ago. The Baghdadi Jews arrived in India around 1730 and eventually included wealthy merchants from throughout the Middle East. Many of them looked down on the B'nai Israel and questioned their Jewish origins. There was also a small Jewish community in Cochin. At its peak in the late 1940s, there were a total of about 26,000 members of the Indian Jewish community, including some European refugees. The large majority of Indian Jews emigrated in the 1950s and 1960s; most of them went to Israel. By the time V. L. Benjamin visited Bombay, there were only about 250 Baghdadis and several thousand B'nai Israel remaining there.

ORT, a Jewish organization that provides education and technical training, had established a branch in Bombay. V. L. Benjamin later sent several members of the community there, including his sister and his son, Joshua, for vocational training. The Bombay Jews also provided him with advice on Jewish practices. He returned to Manipur with Jewish calendars and a pamphlet of Jewish prayers.

"We practiced Judaism as well as possible," says Joshua. "About thirty men prayed in our home every Saturday. We didn't have a ritual slaughterer so there was no kosher meat, but we didn't eat pork and didn't mix milk with meat. The boys and men in the community went to a local doctor, a gentile, to be circumcised. My father said a brief prayer during the operation. Whatever was possible, we tried."

Joshua's father also spread the teachings to other branches of the Church of God. His message, linking the Mizos more closely to the Hebrews of the Bible and to Israel, attracted hundreds of new followers. In 1975, when his wife was sent to a hospital in Aizawl for brain surgery, V. L. visited a congregation in a village north of Aizawl. He was invited to preach, and he told the church members that Judaism was the religion of the Bible, the true religion. He talked about the Jewish way of life and practices, such as circumcision, that members of the Church of God in Manipur had adopted. By the time he returned to preach again the following year, half the congregation was ready to embrace Judaism. When a candidate for Parliament, who also happened to be a surgeon, visited the village a few months later, many of the men and boys asked him to perform circumcisions. The doctor did dozens of them.

Benjamin's followers called themselves the United Jews of Northeastern India. They continued to search for knowledge about Jewish practices and hoped to immigrate to Israel. The Bombay Jewish community, dwindling and divided, had little else to offer them. So in the late 1970s, Benjamin turned for help to the Indian Jews who had settled in Israel. He wrote the Indian Jewish Federation in Jerusalem, saying that he represented people who had descended from the Lost Tribes. The federation sent Jewish prayer shawls and prayer books. One of the Indian Jews, Shimson Shimson, offered more substantial help. Shimson was a manager at the Hebrew University library in Jerusalem and knew Rabbi Eliyahu Avichail from his days as a university rabbi. He showed Benjamin's letter to Avichail.

Avichail, who assists communities such as Villanueva's followers in Peru and descendants of secret Jews in Mexico, has traveled throughout India, Afghanistan, Pakistan, Burma, Thailand, Tibet, and China in search of the Lost Tribes. On a summer day in Jerusalem in 1999, Avichail's portable telephone rings constantly in his book-lined living room that doubles as the office for Amishav, the organization that helps him in his search.

"I exchanged several letters with Benjamin late in 1979 and 1980," Avichail says. "After a year, I understood that they were sincere in their desire to become Jews and serious about their connection to the Lost Tribes."

The legend of the Lost Tribes began in 722 B.C.E. when the Assyrians conquered Israel, the northern kingdom, and exiled the Ten Tribes that lived there—Reuben, Levi, Issachar, Zebulun, Dan, Naphtali, Gad, Asher, Ephraim, and Manasseh. The Assyrians took tens of thousands of captives and resettled them somewhere outside of Israel. In 586 B.C.E., the Babylonians conquered Judah, the southern kingdom, destroyed the Temple in Jerusalem, and dispersed the two remaining tribes, Judah and

Benjamin. Sixty or seventy years later, some descendants of those two tribes returned to ancient Israel and rebuilt the Temple. They are considered to be the ancestors of the Jewish people.

The ten northern tribes exiled by the Assyrians apparently vanished from history. Most scholars conclude that they assimilated into Assyrian society. More than 1,500 years later, in the ninth century, Eldad Ha-Dani, a merchant who claimed he descended from the Lost Tribe of Dan and came from East Africa, revived the legend of the Lost Tribes. Ha-Dani expanded on Talmudic commentary that suggested the Lost Tribes had been trapped inside the banks of the Sambatyon river, which spewed rocks and sand during the week and rested on the Sabbath, the only day Jewish travelers could cross it. Ha-Dani published a journal about his travels to Babylonia, North Africa, and Spain, and spread his claim that descendants of four of the Lost Tribes lived in East Africa.

Ha-Dani's claims were widely accepted as fact by Jewish scholars and were later used by Israeli religious authorities to establish links between Ethiopian Jews and the Lost Tribe of Dan, legitimizing their emigration to Israel under the Law of Return. In the twelfth century, the great Jewish travel writer Benjamin of Tudela reported finding descendants of the Lost Tribes living near Bukhara, now part of Uzbekistan. European intellectuals in the sixteenth and seventeenth centuries speculated that the descendants of the Ten Lost Tribes had become American Indians.

Avichail brought the legend of the Lost Tribes into the modern era. Citing biblical accounts, commentaries, and his own research, he determined that the Lost Tribes had lived in Assyria for nearly three centuries. In 331 B.C.E., after Alexander the Great conquered Persia, the tribes were exiled again, this time to Afghanistan and other countries, where they became shepherds and idol worshipers. When the Muslims conquered these territories, the members of the Lost Tribes were forced to convert to Islam. According to Avichail, some of them migrated east to India, Kashmir, Tibet, and China.

After years of investigation and travels abroad, Avichail believes he has identified millions of lost Jewish souls, people living as non-Jews who are descendants of the Lost Tribes. They include 15 million Pathans, mostly in Afghanistan and Pakistan, 5 to 7 million Kashmiris in territory disputed by India and Pakistan, 1 to 2 million Manasseh on the India-Burmese border, and about 250,000 Chiang-min on China's border with Tibet. Avichail says he has found proof of their origins in Jewish customs they have retained, their racial characteristics, and ancient graves and stones engraved in Hebrew. Some Muslims in Afghanistan, Pakistan, and Kashmir, for example, identify themselves as B'nai Yisrael, the ancient Hebrew name for Children of Israel, and have Semitic features and light skin. The elders recollect practices similar to Jewish rites, including animal sacrifice, lighting candles or lamps on Friday nights, circumcision, and some Jewish dietary restrictions. The names of several Pathan tribes are similar to the names of some of the Lost Tribes.

Most scholars dispute Avichail's conclusions. Historians conclude that the Jews who migrated to Asia were descendants of the Tribes of Judah and Benjamin who arrived after the Second Temple was destroyed (70 C.E.). Some entered Afghanistan and Central Asia along the Silk Road, and others settled in India. The first Jews who reached China possessed texts written in ancient Israel as late as the second century B.C.E., more than 600 years after the Assyrians had exiled the Lost Tribes.

The earliest authentic record of Jews in China dates from the eighth century C.E.; by the beginning of the ninth century, there were about ten Jewish settlements in China. Jews settled in Kaifeng, the ancient Chinese capital, sometime in the late tenth or early eleventh century and built a synagogue there in 1163. It wasn't until 1605 that Westerners first made contact with the Chinese Jews, when Ai T'ien, a member of the Kaifeng community, visited the Jesuit priest Matteo Ricci in Beijing. The Kaifeng Jews, isolated from other Jewish communities, had forgotten most of their beliefs and practices. Ai T'ien assumed Ricci was a Jew since he also believed in one God, although he noted that Ricci mistakenly believed the Messiah had already arrived. Two years later, Ricci sent two Chinese emissaries to visit Kaifeng. They returned with an offer from the Jewish community's aging rabbi: If Ricci would give up his practice of eating pork, he was invited to become Kaifeng's next chief rabbi.

Pan Guandan, perhaps the foremost Chinese historian on Jews in ancient China, wrote that based on the calendar they used and their religious practices, the Jews who settled in Kaifeng left ancient Israel sometime in the second century B.C.E. According to Pan, they later settled near Bombay—perhaps as the B'nai Israel—and lived there for 1,100 years before some of them sailed to China. A few Kaifeng Jews probably emigrated directly from Persia; but none of them, Pan writes, claimed descent from the Lost Tribes of Israel.

To many scholars and rabbis, Avichail's search is not only quixotic but also has little foundation in Jewish law or lore. The biblical prophets predicted that only God or the Messiah could redeem the Lost Tribes. The great sage Rabbi Akiba wrote that the Ten Tribes would never be redeemed, even after the coming of the Messiah, because they had defamed the land of Israel by announcing that their homes in exile were twice as pleasant as in Israel. Avichail cites other sages, however, who believed that the return of the Lost Tribes would hasten the coming of the Messiah and lead to the rededication of the Temple in Jerusalem and an era of peace and prosperity. "It is an accepted tradition," Avichail writes in his book *The Tribes of Israel,* "that in matters of redemption, heavenly intervention will be the result of human initiation. . . . The main redemption of the Ten Tribes will be by the Messiah of the House of David, but we must also act to the best of our ability."

It is unlikely, even with DNA testing, that the legend of the Lost Tribes can be either proven or refuted. Nonetheless, they present a troubling problem for religious authorities, regardless of their true origins: Should they be accepted as Jews?

Writes Avichail:

Since we have no method for examining souls, we reject a gentile who desires to convert until it is proven that his conversion is a sincere one, which proves that his soul has a Jewish origin.

All agree that whoever has a Jewish soul is of Israeli origin and we are commanded to seek him out and return him to the fold. . . . Moreover, even if we have doubts about some of the tribes who exhibit Jewish customs and signs, still we must try to return them, as *halacha* [Jewish law] dictates about one whose Jewishness is in doubt.

This process of returning the tribes must be done after careful examination of facts and people and proper preparation for conversion, after which the true converts should be allowed to join our people.

AVICHAIL TRAVELED TO India for the first time in 1980 to meet with members of the United Jews of Northeastern India. The Indian government refused, however, to grant him a permit to visit Mizoram and Manipur. Both territories were caught up in civil war and had yet to become provinces of India.

Avichail later wrote V. L. Benjamin that the community should select two young men to send to Israel. He promised to train them in Jewish law and ritual and send them back to educate others. The process could take many years, Avichail wrote, and perhaps only a few of them would succeed. At the time, there were about 300 members of the community eager to live in Israel as Jews.

The community selected Gideon Rei and Simon Gyn, both farmers from Churachandpur who had long been members of Benjamin's community. With tourist visas and airplane tickets sent by Avichail, they flew to Tel Aviv in January 1982. They studied Hebrew in a *kibbutz* for ten months and then continued their studies in the West Bank. Rei and Gyn spent more than a year learning Jewish law and practices in Shechem, near the cave where Manasseh's father, Joseph, is buried. In the meantime, several Mizos who had studied at ORT in Bombay came to Israel and were converted there. Others, including Joshua Benjamin, learned trades and received some instruction in Hebrew and Jewish practices at ORT.

Rei and Gyn returned to India after two years of study to become the Mizo community's religious leaders. They transliterated prayer books, including the Passover *Haggadah*, into Mizo, conducted services and religious classes in small synagogues in Mizoram and Manipur, and trained more than 300 people. The congregants now called themselves B'nai Manasseh, Children of Manasseh, and waited for Rabbi Avichail to summon them. In 1985, Avichail came to India with the chief rabbi of Netanya to convene a *bet din*. They met with thirty young people in Bombay who had studied with Rei and Gyn, and questioned them about Judaism and the origins of the Mizos. The rabbi from Netanya was not impressed. He said he didn't believe they descended from the Lost Tribes and agreed to convert only a few of them.

Avichail proceeded slowly. He and other rabbis visited India over the next few years and selected several dozen others for conversion. Twenty-five young people converted in 1988 and came to Israel the following year. Then, in the early 1990s, Israel's Interior Ministry closed the doors.

The prospects for immigration to Israel had become far less favorable in the years since Avichail first had made contact with the Mizo community. By 1993, nearly half a million immigrants from the former Soviet Union, many with questionable ties to Jewish origins, had settled in Israel. They were allowed to enter under a 1970 amendment to the Law of Return that permitted children or grandchildren of Jews, and their spouses and children, to immigrate. More than 45,000 Ethiopian Jews, accepted by rabbinical authorities as descendants of the Lost Tribe of Dan, had arrived in the 1980s and early 1990s, many of them rescued from famine and civil war in a dramatic airlift from Addis Ababa. The handful of Peruvian Jews whom Avichail assisted also had arrived, beginning in 1990.

The legend of the Lost Tribe of Manasseh was now entering the murky realm of Israeli politics. It was up against a simmering controversy over Israel's Law of Return and uneasiness over the recent influx of Jewish immigrants. Both ultra-Orthodox and secular Israeli officials had begun to call for changes in the Law of Return. Chief Rabbi Israel Meir Lau openly questioned the wisdom of welcoming some of the immigrants, including an Ethiopian Jew who was married to eight Christian wives, had seventy-one children, and sought permission to bring his entire family to Israel. The Israeli ambassador to India, in a secret cable to the Foreign Ministry later leaked to the press, had warned that accepting the B'nai Manasseh as Jews could bring millions of new Indian immigrants to Israel. One newspaper headline proclaimed that there were more than 300 million people in the Third World with tenuous ties to Judaism who were waiting to immigrate.

Israel, once a haven for all Jewish immigrants, had become

a prosperous, mostly middle-class society. As the threat of war with the Arabs seemed to recede, some Israelis argued that the new tide of refugees was attracted to Israel for economic reasons.

"We are witnessing a phenomenon that non-Jews are eager to join the Jewish faith if to do so means coming to Israel and upgrading their standard of living," Absorption Minister Yair Tsaban told a foreign reporter in 1994. "We cannot be expected to fulfill all the prophecies of the Bible. We must be willing to leave something for the Messiah to do when He comes."

Without the support of the Israeli government, Avichail looked for guidance from Israel's chief rabbis. He wrote them to ask whether they considered it appropriate to bring a Lost Tribe to Israel and how it should be done. The rabbis did not reply. Then he sent the same questions to Rabbi Schneerson, the Lubavitcher rebbe in Crown Heights. Schneerson replied within three days. He told Avichail to bring more immigrants to Israel, beginning with the unmarried, and to convert them there.

Avichail followed Schneerson's advice, but one additional question remained. Who would finance the flights to Israel? The Jewish Agency, which had paid travel expenses for the Peruvians, refused to assist the B'nai Manasseh without backing from the government. Avichail turned to a retired doctor and financier from Miami who had become a darling of the Israeli right for his efforts to evict Arabs from their homes in Jerusalem.

Dr. Irving I. Moskowitz, an Orthodox Jew born in 1929 in Manhattan, made his fortune by buying hospitals in Southern California beginning in the late 1950s. He later added to his millions by running a giant bingo parlor in Hawaiian Gardens, a small city in Los Angeles County. After the 1967 war in the Middle East, Moskowitz donated funds to help settle immigrants in the newly occupied territories.

Moskowitz's charitable foundation also contributed heavily to Ateret Cohanim (Crown of the Priests), an ultra-Orthodox group that claims Jews have an historic right to Arab property in Jerusalem. Its militant supporters occupied dozens of Arab-owned properties without warning, evicting tenants and defying Israeli police and the courts to challenge them.

Avichail selected forty B'nai Manasseh, unmarried men and women between seventeen and thirty-five, and provided them with tourist visas for Israel. Moskowitz gave each of them $550 for airfare. They arrived in July 1993. Avichail's supporters in the religious nationalist movement, who had welcomed the Peruvians to Eilon Moreh, settled the B'nai Manasseh in Gush Katif, an agricultural community in the Gaza Strip. The Indian immigrants replaced Palestinian laborers in Gaza that the right-wing settlers considered to be security threats. Fifty more Indians arrived the following summer, including, for the first time, several families.

Joshua Benjamin arrived in the summer of 1995. He came with his wife, two children, and his grandmother, the widow of Thankamlova. Joshua's father, V. L. Benjamin, who had first brought modern Jewish practices to the Mizos, had died in 1988, hopeful that his children would eventually settle in Israel.

"I was very happy when I left India," Joshua recalls. "I wasn't worried about my job or how I would feed my family. I was interested only in reaching Israel, to kiss the land. It was so wonderful to see the scenery, the religious people praying." After eight months of study, Joshua and his wife underwent formal conversions, first being questioned by a Jewish court, then being immersed in a *mikvah*.

"The *mikvah* felt like holy water, pure water," Joshua says. "I felt I had cleaned away all the sins of my past; I felt like a new man when the rabbi blessed me."

By 1998, more than 350 B'nai Manasseh had been trained in Jewish practices, converted, and settled in Gaza and the West Bank, where some worked side-by-side with the Peruvians. The immigrants include former physicians, engineers, and lawyers, most of whom now work as manual laborers.

Despite the difficulty of adjusting to life in Israel, hundreds of other B'nai Manasseh hope to emigrate as well. Some of them, particularly in Manipur, have seemingly compelling reasons for leaving.

IN SEPTEMBER 1997, V. P. Yahashua, who identified himself as the secretary of the Manasseh People's Congress in Manipur, sent an urgent letter to Kulanu, the Maryland-based group that had been inspired by Rabbi Avichail's work and had assisted both the Abayudaya in Uganda and Villanueva's followers in Peru. The letter was addressed to Jack Zeller, the president of Kulanu, and reported on fighting between members of two communities, the Kukis and the Paite.

Yahashua wrote from a refugee camp that a hundred persons were killed, fifty were injured, and thousands were homeless.

Yahashua said his group had set up a relief committee, which was seeking charitable contributions, and asked Zeller to circulate word of his community's plight. A few months later, a group of Canadian activists formed the Canadian Friends of the Bnai Menashe to raise funds for the refugees in Manipur. It was headed by Felix Golubev, who had visited Manipur as a producer for filmmaker Simcha Jacobovici's *Quest for the Lost Tribes*, a documentary about the Manasseh and other lost Jews discovered by Avichail.

"We realized that these people are in danger," Golubev told *Maclean's* magazine. "It is urgent."

Golubev's group found support from the Canadian Jewish Congress. The president of the congress, Moshe Ronen, lobbied for the B'nai Manasseh in a meeting with then Israeli prime minister Benjamin Netanyahu, requesting visas for 211 young people from two villages in Manipur that had been attacked. Netanyahu expressed sympathy, Ronen said, but his government, still fearful of a mass influx of Indians, refused to issue the visas.

Jacobovici, who had campaigned on behalf of the Ethiopian Jews in the 1980s and early 1990s, wrote an opinion article for *The Boston Globe*, accusing the Israeli government of indifference in a matter of life and death.

He wrote that according to the B'nai Manasseh, Naga tribesmen "are conducting a campaign of ethnic cleansing against them. The Nagas are using the Manasseh legends of belonging to another homeland as a pretext for driving them out of the hill country. Recently, two synagogues were burned in a Naga-led program in the town of Churachandpur."

The reality in Manipur is a bit more complex, however. Naga guerrillas, fighting to expand the Naga homeland, have killed hundreds of Kukis since 1993, hoping to drive them from the region. The Nagas also formed an alliance with another tribe, the Paites. The Kukis have fought back with their own guerrilla forces. Most of the death and destruction in recent years has in-volved Kukis fighting Paites. It is a political, not a religious, war. Both tribes claim descent from Manasseh and include members who hope to live in Israel. The fighting has been brutal, hun-dreds have been killed, and villages have been burned to the ground. Yet some observers believe that some Paites and Kukis have tried to exploit the conflict so they can emigrate more rapidly. The Paites and Kukis signed a peace agreement in 1998.

AVICHAIL NOW SAYS he is more certain than ever that the B'nai Manasseh are descendants of the Ten Lost Tribes.

"On my first visits to India, I was in doubt if we could even be fifty percent certain," Avichail told me. "The important thing is that their motivation is good and we are obligated to convert them and bring them to Israel. Who can know if they are from the Tribe of Manasseh?

"But when I heard their songs and legends on my last visit to India [in June 1998], I became one hundred percent sure. I am now convinced the Mizos are from the Ten Lost Tribes. It was very, very clear."

The elders tell legends about leaving Zion for the east, to places with names that sound like Afghanistan and the Hi-malayas. They recall that the Mizos lived for many centuries in

China, where they suffered under the rule of the first Chinese emperor, Qin Shihuang, in the third century B.C.E. Qin may have taken them as captives from their previous home and used them as slaves to help build the Great Wall of China. One story relates that their ancestors carried a type of parchment with them—perhaps a Torah scroll—but it was lost in China, possibly eaten by a dog. This may have been a metaphor, how-ever; Qin, who had ordered the burning of nearly all books and scrolls, was often called a dog for his cruel leadership. After Qin's death, according to the legend, the Mizos dispersed throughout China. Some of them later traveled west, to Thai-land, Burma, and northeastern India.

The elders also related Mizo rituals that parallel those of the Hebrews. Some of their customs haven't been practiced by Jews for more than 1,000 years.

"They told us the priests used to perform circumcisions on the eighth day by taking two sharp stones and placing them in a fire to cleanse them," Avichail says. "Someone else held the foreskin while the priest cut it and recited prayers.

"The priests also performed sacrifices for sick people and would cut the neck of a chicken or lamb, drain the blood, and place some on the ear, back, and leg of the sick person. If everyone in the house was sick, the priest would put blood on the doorposts." This practice echoes the way the ancient He-brews painted blood on their doorposts in Egypt to protect their firstborn sons.

When the priests performed sacrifices, they prayed to their god, Pathian, and invoked the name of Manasseh: "Pathian from above, we the sons of Manasseh offer you the blood of animals."

They performed similar sacrifices and prayers before a hunt and in selecting the site for a field or new village. In modern times, if there is some illness or danger, Mizos ask for help from Manasseh.

These are customs from biblical times, Avichail says.

"They also sang about the Passover sacrifice. As in ancient times, the priest would not break the bones of the animal, and would burn its innards on a stone altar. He would bury any meat he didn't eat. It is called *helenkel* in Mizo, a word that means 'pass over.' "

Mizo elders also sang songs that harkened back to biblical times, including a nursery rhyme about Miriam, Moses' sister, who led the Jews through the Red Sea as she played timbrels. At the end of the song, two children hold up their hands to form a gate, and beckon the other children to pass through by singing, "Enter, enter to Zion."

Another song tells the story of the exodus from Egypt:

We had to cross the Red Sea;
Our enemies were coming after us with chariots;
The sea swallowed them as if they are meat;
We are led by fire at night;
Take those birds for food;
And drink water coming out from the rock.

The elders used ancient names for places in Israel, such as Shiloh and Mt. Moriah, Avichail says, and called God Yahweh, His name as it appears phonetically in the Bible. In their songs, they pronounced only the first syllable of His name—in accordance with Jewish tradition not to speak aloud the name of God.

"They sing, 'Answer me, answer me. Hoy ya', Hoy ya'. You are living in Mt. Moriah, in the Red Sea, in Sinai, on Mount Zion.'

"They sang about Terach, Abraham's father, even though they didn't know who he was, and about 'Apram' and 'Yasak' and about the sea closing in on the Egyptians and how they were eaten by fish," Avichail says. "Those things aren't written that way in the Bible. If they were one hundred percent accurate, after being passed down for three thousand years, I would doubt the story and believe it was a copy."

The idea that the Mizos descend from the Lost Tribes remains an intriguing tale. It seems likely, however, that it was first suggested by nineteenth-century Christian missionaries eager to connect Mizo tribal rituals to passages in the Bible and to attract converts. Missionaries in Burma and China made similar connections among tribal peoples there. One clue is that some of the songs recalled by Mizo elders involve characters from the New Testament, including a folktale about Paul, who watched over those passing into the dead man's village.

AFTER TWENTY YEARS of civil war, Mizoram is now the most peaceful region in northeastern India. Aizawl bustles with activity on its narrow, twisting streets that climb and descend gorges and overlook deep riverbanks. It can take hours to travel a short distance in a four-wheel drive truck, negotiating turns so tight that only one vehicle can pass at a time. Nearly all of the houses are supported by stilts and lean over hillsides; a fall out a bedroom window could send someone tumbling down hundreds of feet.

The city center is a chaotic mix of stores and markets selling clothing, fresh meat, small appliances, and cassettes of Western and local music. A handful of tourists stop to photograph the streets and stores that proclaim links to Israel, such as Zion Street and the Israel Store. Churches of all denominations dot the hillsides.

One is Beit Hashem Midrash, House for the Study of God, a messianic church founded by Americans who were raised as Jews but worship Jesus. Like followers of the Church of God in Manipur, its members observe Jewish holidays with Christian rituals. On Passover, while Jews celebrate with a *seder*, the congregants of Beit Hashem Midrash don white outfits and go to church. A guitar player sits cross-legged to greet them near the door, where they remove their shoes. Their priest, called *Cohen* (the Hebrew word for priest), washes their feet and performs the sacrament. The members of the church observe the Sabbath on Saturday, don't eat pork, and are called to services on the first day of the lunar calendar by the sounds of a buffalo horn. The males are required to be circumcised. The congregants have the glassy-eyed look of religious zealots. They, too, yearn for Israel but will wait to go until their Messiah returns.

The Shalom Tsion Synagogue of the Manasseh community is a few streets away, a simple tin structure accessible by a steep, descending stairway. The windows on one side overlook a deep valley. The congregation has rented the building for the last ten years, but the landlord, a Presbyterian, is now trying to sell it.

The day after the *seder* at Jeremiah's house, I attend morning services there. About twenty men, wearing prayer shawls and knitted skullcaps, pray in Hebrew in the front half of the synagogue. An equal number of women and children sit quietly in the back. A handmade wooden ark behind the lectern holds a Torah that Avichail donated. Eliezer Sela, a short, gray-haired man in his late fifties who serves as the religious leader, conducts the service. The melodies and Hebrew pronunciation are based on the Ashkenazic practices that Gideon Rei learned in Israel. Several families recently split with Shalom Tsion to form a congregation that follows the Sephardic practices, maintaining that the Manasseh should be Sephardic if they originated in ancient Samaria.

Eliezer Sela was born in a small village in 1943 and grew up as a Presbyterian. He became a member of the Church of God in 1970, and after he heard V. L. Benjamin speak in 1975 and 1976, he joined other congregants who adopted Jewish practices. He, his wife, Doliani, and their five children learned more about Jewish law and the Torah from Rei in the 1980s. Their children immigrated to Israel in the early 1990s and settled in Kiryat Arba. In 1997, Rabbi Avichail sent Eliezer to Israel for seven months, where he studied to become Rei's replacement.

"I wanted to stay in Israel, but Avichail said I had to return to be the religious leader," Eliezer says with a sad smile after services. "I will be here until someone else comes or is trained to replace me."

Members of the congregation make their own phylacteries, prayer shawls, and skullcaps. There is no ritual bath or trained kosher slaughterer in the community, so some of their practices don't conform to Orthodox Jewish law. They eat some foods during the holiday, like rice, that are not considered kosher for Passover by the Ashkenazic Jews who trained them. Eliezer has a simple explanation for these variations: "It's not the Holy Land," he says.

We have lunch at Eliezer and Doliani's home. The walls are adorned with a photograph of Avichail, a Jewish calendar, and a *seder* plate. I ask Eliezer if he has heard that some Israelis do not welcome their immigration to Israel.

"It is written in the Torah that we will return to Zion," Eliezer replies. "We need to return as soon as possible. We are descendants of Manasseh; the Messiah will come if we practice Judaism."

Is he concerned that his people are being settled on the front lines and face danger from the Arab-Israeli conflict or could lose their homes under proposed peace agreements? His face takes on a faraway look, similar to some of the messianic Jews I had spoken with a few hours earlier.

"I will settle any place, anywhere in Israel," Eliezer says. "I will never complain because we go there not only for this world but for the world to come. The power of God will work, and miracles will come with the new millennium."

The Mizos—also known as Chins and Kukis—were fierce warriors . . . Others would enter the village of the dead, a shadowy underworld. N. E. Parry, *A Monograph on Lushai Customs and Ceremonies* (Aizawl, Mizoram, India: Tribal Research Institute, 1928); C. G. Verghese, *A History of the Mizos* (Mizoram, India: Vikas Press, n.d.).

The missionaries claimed to find similarities . . . They also returned to beliefs in the supernatural.   Meyer Samra, "Judaism in Manipur and Mizoram," *Australian Journal of Jewish Studies* 6, no. 1 (1992).

Like other Christian fundamentalists . . .   Ibid.

The rebellion had begun in 1961 . . . and pursued them into the surrounding villages.   David Abram, Devdan Sen, Harriet Sharkey, and Gareth John Williams, *India: The Rough Guide* (New York: Penguin, 1998), p. 894; Rone Tempest, "Famine Sparked Revolt; Rebel Anger Blooms into Indian State, *Los Angeles Times,* February 25, 1987.

There were actually two separate Jewish communities . . .   Sadok Masliyah, "The Bene Israel and the Baghdadis: Two Indian Jewish Communities in Conflict," *Judaism: A Quarterly Journal of Jewish Life and Thought* 43, no. 3 (1994).

More than 1,500 years later, in the ninth century, Eldad Ha-Dani . . . Nathan Ausubel, ed., *A Treasury of Jewish Folklore* (New York: Crown, 1977), pp. 517–20.

Avichail brought the legend of the Lost Tribes . . .   Rabbi Eliyahu Avichail, *The Tribes of Israel* (Jerusalem: Amishav, 1989).

Historians conclude . . . he was invited to become Kaifeng's next chief rabbi.   Michael Pollack, *Mandarins, Jews, and Missionaries* (Philadelphia: Jewish Publication Society, 1980), p. 255.

Pan Guandan, perhaps the foremost Chinese historian . . .   Sidney Shapiro, ed. and trans., *Jews in Old China* (New York: Hippocrene, 1988), pp. 46–92.

By 1993, nearly half a million immigrants . . .   Clyde Haberman, " 'Lost Tribe' Has Israelis Pondering Law of Return," *New York Times,* October 6, 1994, p. A3.

Both ultra-Orthodox and secular Israeli officials . . .   Herb Keinon, "Make Room for the Remnants of the Lost Tribes," *Jerusalem Post,* September 2, 1994, p. 1B.

. . . there were more than 300 million people . . .   Haberman, " 'Lost Tribe.' "

"We are witnessing a phenomenon . . ."   Keinon, "Make Room."

. . . Avichail looked for guidance from Israel's chief rabbis.   Haim Shapiro, " 'Lost Tribe' Group to Replace Arab Workers and Convert," *Jerusalem Post,* July 30, 1993.

Dr. Irving I. Moskowitz, an Orthodox Jew . . .   Patrick Cockburn, *South China Morning Post* (reprinted from *The Independent* [London]), September 20, 1997, p. 21; Joel Greenberg, "The Israeli Vote: The Settlers; On the Shaken Right, a First-Day Challenge," *New York Times,* May 19, 1999, p. A13.

Avichail selected forty B'nai Manasseh . . .   Shapiro, " 'Lost Tribe' Group."

The Indian immigrants replaced Palestinian laborers . . .   Michael S. Arnold, "Menashe's Children," *Jerusalem Post,* March 13, 1998, p. 12.

In September 1997, V. P. Yahashua . . .   Copy of letter supplied by Rabbi Jacques Cukierkorn.

"We realized that these people are in danger" . . .   Nomi Morris, "The Jews of Asia: Canadians Urge Israel to Aid a 'Lost Tribe,' " *Maclean's,* August 10, 1998, p. 27.

. . . accusing the Israeli government of indifference . . .   Simcha Jacobovici, "A 'Lost Tribe' Tries to Return," *Boston Globe,* August 17, 1998, p. A11.

Qin may have taken them as captives . . .   Zaithanchhungi, *Israel-Mizo Identity,* Aizawl, Mizoram, India: J. R. Bros Offset Printers, 1994).

Chapter Four

AMAZON FLOWERS

It seems, at first, to be an unremarkable event, the celebration of Abraham Benmoyal's fiftieth birthday. The party takes place in Benmoyal's neat, two-story home in a middle-class neighborhood. Two German shepherds bark ferociously next door, restrained by a tall stockade fence. The guests in the dining room munch on *coxinha*—a Brazilian snack of fried dough with chicken inside—and small, layered sandwiches filled with sliced fish. A dozen young people sprawl on the rug in the adjoining living room, wrestling, flirting, and watching *The Silence of the Lambs*, dubbed in Portuguese, on a large color television. A chocolate sheet cake, covered with birthday candles, has been placed on the long dining room table.

Yet this is Manaus, in the center of the Brazilian Amazon, where nothing is as simple as it seems.

The host is a tall, amiable man with a neat gray-and-white beard, the director of the local Jewish burial society. He owes his position, one of some importance in the status-conscious Sephardic community, at least in part to an extraordinary ancestor. Shalom Moyal, his great-uncle, was a rabbi from Israel who after his death was worshiped as a holy man by both Christians and Jews.

In 1910, Rabbi Moyal came to Manaus to raise money for his school in Jerusalem. At the time, this small Jewish community was among the wealthiest in the world. Hundreds of poor Jews from northern Morocco, and thousands of non-Jewish immigrants from Europe, had made their fortunes in the Amazon rubber boom late in the nineteenth century. The neoclassical Manaus opera house, designed by an Italian architect and fashioned from pink granite and Italian marble in 1896, became a symbol of those prosperous years.

Rabbi Moyal's fund-raising trip ended in tragedy. He died of an unknown illness on March 12, 1910, not long after he arrived. There wasn't a separate Jewish cemetery at the time, so he was buried in the middle of a vast Christian cemetery, a few blocks from the opera house. His family came from Israel the following year to return his body to Jerusalem. But his remains never left the Amazon.

According to local legend, the gravedigger who tried to disinter the body was paralyzed as he put a shovel in the rabbi's grave. Since then, Rabbi Moyal has been revered throughout northern Brazil and the Amazon, and thousands of people visit his grave each year. When I visit, his tomb, engraved in Hebrew and Portuguese, is covered with white, pink, and yellow roses; beads; candles; coins; and dozens of small pebbles. A few messages scrawled on small pieces of paper, pleading for the rabbi's help with a sick child or ailing grandparent, are scattered among the pebbles and flowers. Small plaster plaques thanking the rabbi for his kindnesses hang from a low blue stone wall enclosing the grave.

Catholics call him Saint Rabbi Moyal and believe he has magical powers. Descendants of Moroccan Jews who live here venerate him as a *tzaddik,* a pious man who even after his death can perform miracles, such as curing the sick or rescuing someone from danger.

But Benmoyal's party, which brings young people in their teens and early twenties together with leaders of the local synagogue and older couples, is not simply a birthday gathering; it is also a celebration of the revival of Jewish life in the Amazon.

The young people belong to a class of twenty-five who are being trained in Judaism, studying mysticism and Torah, and participating in social activities like this one. Nearly all of them are descendants of Moroccan Jews who came to the Amazon two or three generations ago and whose families have lost touch with their traditions. There are now as many as 50,000 descendants of Moroccan Jews living in communities along the Amazon. Since the mass migration of most of Morocco's 300,000 Jews to Israel in the 1950s and 1960s, Manaus—along with Belém at the mouth of the Amazon—is now among the few places in the world where some facets of ancient Moroccan Jewish life survive.

JAIME BENCHAYA IS one of the guests at Benmoyal's party. He has fair skin, a thick gray-and-white beard, and a ready, youthful smile. He wears jeans and a plaid cotton shirt with the sleeves rolled up past his elbows. After the party, accompanied by his wife, Margarida, and several guests, he drives me in his red Ford Mustang convertible to a nearby ice cream shop, where we talk.

"My ancestors ran away from difficulties in Morocco and became adventurers and successful traders," Benchaya tells me between spoonfuls of vanilla ice cream. "But it was only men who came, and they didn't pass on their Jewish practices."

Jews had lived in Morocco since the destruction of the Second Temple in 70 C.E., when exiles from ancient Israel converted a large number of Moroccan Berber tribes to Judaism. It later became a refuge for Jews who faced persecution in Spain, first under the Visigoths in the seventh century and later in the fifteenth century after King Ferdinand and Queen Isabella ordered that all Jews convert to Christianity or be killed.

Benchaya's ancestors fled from Spain to Morocco in the middle of the fifteenth century. They most likely settled just across the Strait of Gibraltar in Tangier, where they would have worked as tailors, cobblers, or peddlers and lived in a small apartment in the *mellah,* the crowded Jewish quarter. Jews in the *mellah* were protected by the nearby sultan and guaranteed political autonomy, property rights, and religious freedom. They were taxed heavily, however, and the living conditions were miserable. "The houses are leprous, the ground is muddy, and filth in the dark and narrow lanes is repulsive," a French visitor wrote in the 1880s. "Long lines of beggars fill the streets, assailing the passersby with their wailing, displaying their clothes in shreds, their sores covered in vermin, or asleep dressed in their torn burnooses in the dust and refuse which have accumulated alongside the houses."

The Benchaya family eventually resettled in Casablanca, a city along the Atlantic coast that was destroyed and rebuilt by the Portuguese in the fifteenth and sixteenth centuries and became a center of industry and foreign trade as well as one of the world's largest ports. They worked as traders, prospering under the monopoly over sugar exports the Saadian rulers had granted to the Jews, exchanging sugar for cloth and guns from Europe. Jews were still taxed heavily, but the Benchayas accumulated enough wealth and status to have a synagogue in Casablanca named in their honor.

They worshiped there three times a day, with each service including readings from the Zohar, the basic text of Jewish mysticism that was central to Moroccan Jewish life. The Zohar provides commentary on the Hebrew Bible as well as philosophical explorations of the nature of God, the destiny of man, and the meaning of evil. Its disciples use numerology and other techniques to unearth the hidden messages of the Bible.

The Benchayas, like other Sephardic Jews in Morocco, spoke Haketia, a mixture of Spanish, Hebrew, and Arabic. They adopted some customs and practices from the Arabs and the Berber Jews, wearing talismans—such as the evil eye and necklaces made of gloves—to protect them from demons and to ward off witches and other spirits. Sephardic cooking assimilated Arab herbs and spices, which were valued as aphrodisiacs and for their therapeutic and magical qualities. In their cuisine, the Sephardis combined sweet and sour flavors from their Persian origins—such as meats cooked with fruit—with dishes they adapted from their Arab neighbors—such as *harissa*, a porridge of wheat and meat flavored with melted fat and cinammon, and semolina sweets with dates.

Yet the Benchayas and most other Sephardis continued to think of themselves as Europeans, even after living in Morocco for hundreds of years. They considered themselves superior to the Berber Jews, who tended to be poorer and less educated. Many Sephardis studied at the Alliance Israelite Universelle, a French school for Jewish children that opened branches in Morocco in the 1860s.

The Alliance school introduced new ideas from Europe; perhaps the most influential was the concept, popular among European Jews at the time, that Jews could succeed as laborers as well as intellectuals. This belief took hold in Morocco as political and economic conditions deteriorated in the middle of the nineteenth century. In a country that had been ravaged by battles between the French and the Spanish, a cholera epidemic, and famine, Jews encountered increasing hostility from Arab leaders as well as French and Spanish diplomats. Young people faced a weak job market and an uncertain future.

Some of the younger generation decided to leave Morocco, following another Sephardic tradition. For centuries, their ancestors had been immigrating to foreign lands, from Israel to Persia, from Spain to North Africa and throughout the Ottoman empire. As they traveled and worked abroad, most Moroccan Jews remained close to their families and community and often returned to celebrate Passover. In the nineteenth century, many left for other parts of Africa, the United States, and South America, hoping to bring back newfound riches.

The most promising opportunities seemed to be in South America, where Spanish and Portuguese cultures and languages predominated. The earliest immigrants to Brazil, many of whom brought their families, arrived shortly after Brazil declared independence. They founded a Jewish community in Belém, near the mouth of the Amazon river, and built a synagogue there in 1824 called the Synagogue Porta do Céu, Gates of Heaven. The number of Moroccan immigrants remained small until 1866, when the Booth Line began regular steamship service between Europe and northern Brazil, cutting the travel time from three months to three weeks. Over the next few decades, hundreds more Moroccan Jews, nearly all of them single men, set off for Brazil.

The first Moroccan Jewish immigrants founded trading companies in Belém, as they had done in Morocco, dealing in textiles and produce. As jobs became scarce in the city, the newer immigrants journeyed into the Amazon to establish trading posts with the Indians. They settled throughout the world's largest river basin, from Belém to Iquitos, Peru, nearly 2,000 miles inland, and along the hundreds of tributaries that spread over more than one-third of Brazil and parts of Peru.

Most of the Amazon is impenetrable jungle. Its high canopy is formed by hardwood trees where toucans, sloths, and spider monkeys live; jaguars, peccaries, boa constrictors, and anacondas inhabit the shrubs below. The river's edge, covered with rubber trees, is home to alligators, caimans, tapirs, and turtles; and the river itself and its tributaries teem with river dolphins, manatees, piranha, and pirarucu. The immigrants wrote colorful letters to their families about this remarkable world, so different from the suffocating ghettos in Morocco.

They found new opportunities for wealth as well. By the end of the nineteenth century, the rubber tree, native to the Amazon tropics, had launched an economic boom in Brazil. The Indians had long known how to tap the trees, which produced a yellowish, spongy sap. And in 1839, Charles Goodyear developed a process to make the natural rubber durable. Fifty years later, John Dunlop patented the pneumatic rubber tire, spurring the growth of the automobile industry and a worldwide demand for rubber.

The Jewish traders served as intermediaries, canoeing along the river to trade clothes, medicine, and tobacco with the Indians for rubber and other goods. In the small towns that served as trading posts, such as Cametá, Manaus, Maués, Parintins, and Tefé, they also founded small Jewish communities.

Solomon Benchaya, Jaime's grandfather, sailed with his brother and sister from Casablanca via Portugal and arrived in the Amazon near the turn of the twentieth century. They lived first in Belém, where the family collected local products such as Brazil nuts and sold them to trading companies, most of them owned by Jews. As the rubber boom spread, Solomon set off to do his own trading. He settled in Maués, along the Madeira river more than 600 miles west of Belém and nearly 200 miles east of the rapidly expanding port of Manaus.

Maués was untamed wilderness, a frontier town with flat white beaches along a clear, slow-moving river. Solomon Benchaya bought knives, cooking pots, and cloth from visiting merchants, usually fellow Moroccan Jews, then hired an Indian guide to canoe with him into the jungle. He often spent months along the river collecting rubber in large wooden barrels, and then returned to Maués to exchange it for credit and a fresh supply of goods to barter.

In the jungle, it was easy for even an experienced guide to get lost among the winding rivers and giant trees that blocked the sun. The climate was unremittingly hostile. The temperature averaged about 85 degrees, but the high humidity soaked through clothes during the day and through blankets at night. Sudden and violent rainstorms flooded canoes and washed supplies and passengers into the river. Jaguars sometimes wandered to the riverbank at night, tearing open tents or knocking down huts in search of food. Poisonous snakes, like the brown and grayish fer-de-lance, hid among the bushes, striking quickly and silently. In the river, huge tapirs could easily tip over and sink a canoe. Mosquitoes carried malaria, yellow fever, and other deadly diseases. Some of the most delicious-looking fruits and berries contained fatal toxins.

When he camped along the riverbanks, Solomon Benchaya was often greeted by Indians with painted faces who spoke languages he didn't recognize. The guides translated as best they could, but much of the communication was through crude sign language. Most of the Indians brought rubber, quinine, vanilla, cocoa, and other crops to trade, and offered cures for illnesses that a foreigner was likely to contract. A few were less welcoming; the most hostile tribes attacked visitors with poisonous blow darts.

At some of the Indian villages, Solomon Benchaya occasionally met young men with names such as Assayag, Benchimol, Cohen, and Pinto, fellow Moroccan Jews who also had come to trade. They exchanged stories from the jungle and from home, reconnecting with Moroccan Jewry amid one of the most remote and isolated places on earth. If it was the Sabbath or a Jewish holiday, they would pray together, unrolling their musty skullcaps and prayer shawls from their packs. When Yom Kippur, the Day of Atonement, approached, the traders stopped work, sought one another out, fasted, and prayed. One of the Moroccan Jews in the Amazon, Abraham Pinto, wrote in his journal in the 1890s:

Lest we forget the religion of our fathers so far away, each of us left Tangier carrying with us the Book of Kippur in order to celebrate this day as it should be. Before leaving Tefé for whatever part, we fixed the date of the Holy Day to celebrate it wherever we might be . . . and planned to meet two or three days beforehand to celebrate together. [On meeting], our oarsmen built us a little hut in a place cut out of the jungle. We lit a bonfire and fed it through the night to keep away wild animals and snakes that might come near.

When they were back in port, the Jews prayed together each Sabbath. In Maués, Solomon Benchaya prayed with as many as twenty other men at the home of Moses Abecassis, who came from Tangier. Isaac Abouabe, a strange, reclusive man who had served as a rabbi in Morocco, led the services. All of the men found it difficult to follow Jewish practices in the Amazon. It was impossible to find kosher meat, and none of the young men in Maués had been trained as a kosher butcher. In the jungle, they didn't closely follow biblical decrees to eat only fish with fins, scales, and gills, and animals with cloven hooves that chew their cud. They ate whatever fish or animals they or their guides could catch and kill.

Yet they continued to be loyal to their parents back home, sending money to build new houses or to pay for a brother's or sister's education. Many of the young men returned to Morocco with their newfound wealth after seven or eight years in the Amazon. Others remained in the Amazon and gradually assimilated. They set up households with local girls, barely in their teens, whose milk-chocolate skin, straight dark hair, and small noses identified them as a *caboclas*, the Brazilian term for women of mixed African, Indian, and European blood. Even Rabbi Abouabe lived with a *cabocla*.

The men often lived with three or four different *caboclas*, one in each of the ports they visited between trips into the jungle. After a while, they began to raise families. The *caboclas* considered them to be good providers, even though they left for long periods of time to work in the jungle and stay with their other families. It was not unusual for one man to father two dozen children—giving many of them Jewish names—with four different mothers.

Solomon Benchaya set up a household in Maués with Maria

Patachao. They had six children. The first three had Jewish names, the last three Christian ones: Esther, Moses, and Samuel, then Jaime (Jaime Junior's father), Flora, and Mary. Solomon had girlfriends and families in other ports but never discussed them with his family in Maués. He would leave for months at a time to collect goods, trade with Indians in the jungle, and visit his other families, then return with gifts for Maria and all the children.

Maria had been raised as a Catholic, and she baptized Jaime Sr. and her other children. The family worshiped in church together when Solomon was away; the children attended a Catholic school, the only school in Maués. Solomon seemed to give up hope of sustaining Jewish life in the jungle. He continued to pray at the Abecassis house but made no effort to pass his religion on to his children.

Jaime Sr., who was born in 1918, nonetheless tried to follow some of his father's traditions. As a boy, he prayed with other Moroccan Jews on the Sabbath and holidays even when his father was away, and he regularly read a Portuguese translation of the Hebrew Bible. Like his father, he didn't celebrate the Christian holidays. He fasted on Yom Kippur, didn't eat bread on Passover, and refused to eat pork.

NOT LONG AFTER Jaime Sr. was born, the Amazon rubber trade began its decline. After nearly four decades of prosperity, Brazil lost its monopoly in the world rubber market. The boom collapsed after an Englishman, Henry Alexander Wickham, smuggled rubber seeds out of the port in Belém.

He planted them in British colonies in Southeast Asia, where the British established large rubber plantations. Wickham was later knighted by King George V; Brazilian rubber barons dubbed him the "Executioner of the Amazon." By the 1920s, the British plantations had flooded the market and the price of rubber plummeted.

Most of the remaining Jewish merchants in the Amazon left for home or for new adventures. Those who stayed pursued new trades. Solomon Benchaya opened a dry-goods store in Maués. From a pier behind his house, he exchanged goods with the traders from Belém. He sold them Brazil nuts, jute, and *guaraná*, a highly valued powder ground from seeds that is believed to have restorative and aphrodisiac powers, in return for sugar, beans, rice, and salt from Europe. He sold the imported goods to the locals and Indians from the jungle, mostly on credit. Solomon charged a high interest rate, which was the source of much of his income.

The tales are similar in other towns along the Amazon and its tributaries. Parintins, an island town 100 miles downriver from Maués, was home to dozens of Moroccan Jews, including the Assayags, Cohens, and Sicsus. Simon Elias Assayag was born in Tetuan in 1909 and moved to the Amazon as the rubber boom was coming to an end. He worked as a trader and married a Jewish woman from Belém. He also had several *cabocla* wives and families.

His eldest son from his Jewish wife, Elias Simon, was born upriver in Santarém and grew up in Parintins. Elias mastered many trades. He built the first sailboats in Parintins and also manufactured soap and paint, raised cattle, ran a dry-goods store, served as justice of the peace, and owned the local movie house. Elias had eighteen children with many wives, none of them Jewish. All of his children were baptized. Two sons, José and Simon, still live in Parintins.

José, a building contractor and Elias's oldest son, lives near the center of town, a few blocks from a huge stadium shaped like a bull. Tens of thousands of Brazilians congregate in the stadium for three days each June to watch *caboclas* dressed in Indian costumes dance on colorful floats to drumbeats and songs that celebrate Indian myths. The festival, known as *boi bumbá*, is the source of some of Brazil's most popular folk music, a blend of Indian, Portuguese, African, and Andean melodies. Another of Elias's sons, David, composes popular songs based on *boi bumbá* and is famous throughout Brazil.

José also maintains the Parintins Jewish cemetery. Located across the road from a Catholic church and enclosed by a six-foot-high spiked iron fence, it contains sixty-seven neatly kept graves. The gravestones, inscribed in Portuguese and Hebrew with Moroccan Jewish names such as Assayag, Mendes, Dray, Cohen, Gagy, and Abecassis, rest horizontally on two- to three-foot-high whitewashed slabs that protect the stones from the daily flood of rain. A few small gravestones, for babies who died before they were named or circumcised, are unmarked. The oldest grave, for Donna Cohen, is from 1886; the most recent, for Elias Assayag, is from 1980. Although he had lost touch with Judaism later in life, as Elias neared death he requested that he be buried by Isaac Dahan, then the religious leader of the synagogue in Manaus. Dahan arrived the day after Elias died to recite the Hebrew prayers, wrap the body in a shroud, and help place it in the grave with Elias's feet facing east toward Jerusalem. There hasn't been a Jewish funeral in Parintins since.

JAIME BENCHAYA SR. moved from Maués to Manaus when he was fourteen, volunteering to work at a British-run electric plant, where he learned to repair machinery. He later apprenticed as a mechanic's helper. He returned to Maués five years later to work as an engineer and trader. At age nineteen, he married a *cabocla*, Nadie Michiles; their six children, five girls and Jaime Jr., were baptized, raised as Catholics, and attended Catholic school.

Despite their assimilation and the large number of families with Jewish names, the children sometimes felt that hostility was directed toward them. Teachers often didn't call on the Assayags and Benchayas when they raised their hands in class, and their grades suffered, although they worked as hard and were as bright as the other children. At times their classmates taunted them in the schoolyard.

It wasn't the first time that anti-Semitism had surfaced in the Amazon. The earliest Moroccan Jewish immigrants had confronted age-old stereotypes; occasionally even the most honest businessmen were accused of adulterating their produce and exploiting the Indians. As Jewish life faded in Maués and elsewhere in the Amazon, anti-Semitism remained, emerging in times of surging nationalism, war, and economic crisis.

Anti-Semitism flourished among Brazilian intellectuals in the 1930s, partially in response to the growth of the Communist

movement in Brazil and its purported links to Jews. The Brazilian press openly criticized Jews and called for an end to Jewish immigration. In 1937, the government barred all Jews,
including tourists and businessmen, from entering the country.
Attacks on Jews were common, particularly by German sym-
pathizers on the eve of World War II. In some towns in the
Amazon, the locals looted Jewish stores and chased Jewish families from their homes.

In the early 1940s, when Solomon Benchaya was in his sixties, three Italian teenagers from Maués charged into his house,
blaming Jews for the failing fortunes of the German and Italian armies during World War II. One of the boys brandished
a large pair of tweezers and threatened to pull out Solomon's
fingernails. Solomon fled into the jungle and hid for weeks in
the forest. By the time he returned, the boys had discovered
other distractions. Solomon died of natural causes just before
the end of World War II.

JAIME JR. WAS born in 1950, five years after his grandfather died. He went to the Catholic school in Maués and
worked in his father's store, selling chocolate and other goods.
By the time he was thirteen, he was driving a truck and making deliveries for his father. He started dating Margarida, from
a Catholic family in Maués, in 1967, when he was seventeen
and she was fourteen.

"My family did not accept our relationship when it first
started," says Margarida, a slim, dark-haired woman who now
works as a lawyer for the Treasury Department in Manaus.

"There was some prejudice, but I don't know why my parents didn't want us to be together. Perhaps it was because I was too young, but maybe it was because Jaime was seen as different, his family was different."

They saved money for nearly ten years and were married in 1976, when they were financially independent and could marry without the approval of Margarida's family. A year later, they moved to Manaus. Jaime passed the banking examination and went to work as a treasurer for the Amazonas State Bank. Margarida attended law school and raised their two daughters, Rachel and Sarah. Her parents eventually accepted her marriage.

Shortly after Sarah was born, in 1981, Jaime's father fell ill and could no longer run his business. Jaime decided to move the family back to Maués. With his business and banking skills, he became a successful entrepreneur. At first he ran his father's dry-goods store during the day and drove a truck in the evenings, transporting goods. He soon expanded into farming and mining. During the three-month growing season, he harvested *guaraná* in the jungle, pounded the hard seeds into a powder, and sold it in packages throughout the Amazon.

Jaime also worked in the gold mines in the jungle for a brief time but returned to Manaus after he contracted jungle malaria. In a coma, with dangerously high fevers, he hovered near death for almost a year. After he recovered, he pursued more conventional trades. He ran a bar in Maués and served as the local agent for the *jogo do bicho,* a numbers game that flourishes throughout Brazil. In the big cities, the *jogo,* a lottery using animals instead of numbers that originally raised money for the

Rio de Janeiro zoo, is protected by organized crime and pay-offs to police, but according to Jaime, that is not the case in Maués. Nonetheless, when Abraham Levy, Jaime's partner, managed the *jogo* for him, he took on the appearance of a local hood. Levy strutted around Maués wearing wraparound sunglasses, gold jewelry, and open-necked silk shirts, accompanied by a bodyguard. After he was embarrassed by a Brazilian documentary on Jews in the Amazon that showed him counting money from the *jogo,* Levy gave up the gambling business.

Jaime stayed above the fray and became something of a celebrity. He sponsored a local soccer team, the Sports Club of Maués, and bought uniforms and equipment for the players. He also dabbled in politics.

Local politics in Maués is dominated by entrenched political parties and a network of political patronage. Jaime didn't have connections with the political establishment, but he knew he could draw on a large Jewish vote. Nearly one-third of Maués's population descends from Moroccan Jews. He ran as a candidate for the worker's party, a left-wing group that was believed to have ties to radical organizations and that openly supported the Palestinian Liberation Organization.

"It was the only party that wasn't controlled by old leadership, and they needed candidates," Jaime says. "It may seem strange for a Jew to run for office with a group that backs the PLO, but I don't support that. I just needed a party that could challenge the established powers."

In 1992, Jaime ran for mayor and spent more than $150,000 in his election campaign. He placed third. Two years later, he lost his bid for the provincial legislature. Finally, in 1996, he was elected deputy mayor of Maués. As part of his campaign, Jaime distributed a wallet-sized calendar with his picture on one side; his thumb is pointed up and he is wearing a broad smile. The slogan reads, "Merry Christmas and a prosperous New Year . . . Jamico."

TODAY THERE ARE few signs of Jewish life in Maués. The Jewish cemetery here, unlike the well-kept graveyard in Parintins, lies in a muddy field behind the Christian cemetery, inside a low, uneven wall built from stacks of orange concrete blocks. There are only eight Jewish graves, dating from 1932 to 1984, including one for Solomon Benchaya and another for a Catholic woman who was buried beside her husband. Several of the headstones are cracked. The grave of Rabbi Abouabe, who had prayed with Jaime's grandfather, is covered with dirt and rocks, and his tombstone is broken into a half-dozen pieces. He had suffered from depression and disappeared into the jungle in 1971 when he was well into his nineties. His body was found just outside of town and was brought to the cemetery for burial.

Ruth Benchaya, one of Jaime's older sisters, lives not far from the cemetery. She has remained a practicing Catholic, although she respects her brother's decision to return to Judaism. "The legacy of the Jews here was as founders of Maués, the first traders and shopkeepers," says Ruth, a somber woman with short dark hair. "Jews were always respected by other people here. But they couldn't maintain their religion. Now there are no more Jews here. The only thing that remains are the gravestones and the Jewish names."

IN POLITICS AND in his family life, Jaime Benchaya considers himself to be different, a descendant of Jews who assimilated into Christian culture. Until he was forty-five, he never had been to a synagogue, even when he lived in Manaus, and never had celebrated a Jewish holiday. He remembered almost nothing about Jewish practices. He made no effort to pass on what little he knew to his children. Yet it was his children, Sarah and Rachel, and his non-Jewish wife, Margarida, who tried to bring him back to the religion he had never known.

"I always asked myself why my grandfather stayed in Maués," says Sarah, now enrolled in a premedical program in southern Brazil. "My grandfather was very religious, attached to his family's roots, but in Maués there was no opportunity to live a religious life."

Sarah tells me that she took an interest in Jewish life when she was seven years old and attending a Catholic school in Manaus.

"When I was in first grade, I always enjoyed reading the Book of Psalms. I was always interested in the Jewish religion and the history of the Jewish people. It's very beautiful. I read how the Jewish people had suffered, how they struggled to overcome obstacles, how they were always falling and then getting back up on their feet. That was what attracted me," she says.

At school, a Jewish friend's mother invited her to go to the

Jewish club, Hebraica, a regular gathering place for Jewish families, where Sarah and her girlfriend started taking Hebrew and religious lessons together. The congregation in Manaus follows strict Orthodox ritual.

"Our liturgy, our way of singing and chanting the Torah, is frozen in time," says Isaac Dahan, now president of the synagogue. "It's the same as it was when our ancestors started coming from Morocco. Many of us still speak Haketia, and we still celebrate the birthday of Maimonides' father, like other Moroccan Jews. We eat Jewish Moroccan foods, such as our own version of couscous."

Yet despite their Orthodox practices, Dahan says, Jewish leaders in Manaus have welcomed converts, most of them descendants of Moroccan Jews who had intermarried and abandoned Jewish practices. The last permanent rabbi in Manaus encouraged conversion for anyone who adopted Jewish beliefs and practices. He died in 1976, but since then liberal rabbis from elsewhere in South America have come almost every year to interview candidates and perform conversions for those who are qualified. There have been about thirty conversions in recent years.

"The symbol of our synagogue is a Star of David growing out of an Amazon flower," Dahan says. "We have had a high intermarriage rate, and for many years our community was in decline. But we now have one hundred and sixty Jewish families. The community is reviving, searching for our Jewish traditions. It has been inspired by the young people. It is the children of the intermarried—this is the beauty of the thing—who are the ones seeking Jewish roots."

In 1996, the community hired Abraham Elmescany to serve as a *shaliach,* a teacher who has not been ordained as a rabbi. He is very careful about whom he selects to study with him.

"The religious syncretism in Brazil poses some special problems," Elmescany says to me. "There are evangelicals here who wear skullcaps, learn Hebrew, and believe the State of Israel was established for Jesus. They are plotting to win over and convert Jews. And we have Jews who belong to African cults who make animal sacrifices. So I have to check very carefully on people's motivations for studying and converting.

"I had one woman study with me for a year. When a rabbi came to interview her for a conversion, he asked her whom she believed in. She said she believed in Jesus. So he sent her back for more study. Another woman converted because her husband was Jewish. But a year later, as she lay dying, she called for a priest."

Sarah and Rachel Benchaya participated in Elmescany's study group and socialized with other children who had descended from Moroccan Jews but whose families were no longer practicing as Jews. Margarida encouraged them. They lit Sabbath and holiday candles together in their home, and attended Friday-night services at the synagogue nearly every weekend. Jaime rarely joined them.

"My mother is more Jewish than all the rest of us in the family," Sarah tells me. "She is the one who continuously pushes us toward Judaism."

Margarida says she immediately felt comfortable in the synagogue even though she has no Jewish roots.

"I like the people, the place, the community," Margarida says. "It is part of my daughters' lives so it is part of my life, too."

Margarida's parents and siblings no longer question her interest in Judaism. "They don't consider me a Catholic anymore," she says. "They refer to Judaism as 'your religion.' "

When Sarah was sixteen and Rachel eighteen, they completed their conversions and joined eleven other girls to prepare for a *bat mitzvah* ceremony, signifying their commitment to live Jewish lives. At the Sabbath service four days before Christmas, the girls sang Hebrew prayers, read passages from the Torah, and received the blessings of the congregation. At a reception at Hebraica following the service, Isaac Dahan sang, and guests danced to Jewish music and songs from *boi bumbá*.

In recent years, Jaime has become more interested in Judaism and regularly reads Jewish novels and magazines. He fasts on Yom Kippur and joins his family at the community *seder*s on Passover.

In just three generations, the Benchaya family has lost and regained its Jewish heritage.

In 1910, Rabbi Moyal came to Manaus . . .   Marlise Simons, "Manaus Journal: In the Amazon, Amazing Doings at Rabbi's Tomb," *New York Times,* June 12, 1987, p. A4; Pedro Guerrero, "From Jerusalem Rabbi to Amazon Saint," *Jerusalem Post,* September 27, 1992.

There are now as many as 50,000 descendants . . .   Warren Hoge, "Jews in Brazil Voice Anxiety on Identities," *New York Times,* October 30, 1983, p. A9.

. . . where they would have worked as tailors, cobblers, or peddlers . . . Susan Gilson Miller, "Kippur on the Amazon," in *Sephardi and Middle Eastern Jewries,* Harvey E. Goldberg, ed. (Bloomington, IN: Indiana University Press, 1996), pp. 190–209.

"The houses are leprous . . . accumulated alongside the houses." Pascal Saisset, in "Heures Juives au Maroc," quoted in André N. Chouraqui, *Between East and West: A History of the Jews of North Africa* (Philadelphia: Jewish Publication Society, 1968), p. 124.

Sephardic cooking assimilated Arab herbs and spices . . . Claudia Roden, *The Book of Jewish Food* (New York: Knopf, 1998), pp. 212–14.

Many Sephardis studied at the Alliance . . . hundreds more Moroccan Jews, nearly all of them single men, set off for Brazil. Miller, "Kippur on the Amazon."

. . . in 1839, Charles Goodyear . . . Andrew Draffen, Chris McAsey, Leonardo Pinheiro, and Robyn James, *Brazil: A Lonely Planet Travel Survival Kit,* 3rd ed. (Oakland, CA: Lonely Planet Publications, 1996), pp. 621–23.

They exchanged stories from the jungle and from home . . . One of the Moroccan Jews in the Amazon, Abraham Pinto . . . Miller, "Kippur on the Amazon."

The boom collapsed after an Englishman . . . Draffen et al., *Lonely Planet,* p. 23.

Anti-Semitism flourished among Brazilian intellectuals . . . from entering the country. Jeff Lesser, *Welcoming the Undesirables: Brazil and the Jewish Question* (Berkeley: University of California Press, 1995), pp. 83, 142.

Chapter Five

SECRET JEWS

The young men in the sanctuary, most of them dark-skinned and bearded, chant and rock back and forth to the melody as they sing the words in Hebrew, praising the Torah: "It is a tree of life to those who hold it fast." Most wear prayer shawls over their shoulders; a few have long side curls, commonly worn by ultra-Orthodox Jewish men. In the balcony overhead, four women, their heads covered with scarves, mouth the words silently.

They are praying in a synagogue hidden among the cobble-stoned streets and alleys of the old center of Recife, a coastal city in northeastern Brazil. From the narrow street outside, it appears to be abandoned, a whitewashed stone building with an iron Star of David over the entrance, concealed behind a metal gate, across the street from a tattoo parlor.

Inside, it is hot and musty. A fan attached to one wall barely rustles the fading blue velvet curtain that hangs before the ten-foot-high ark containing the Torah. In the middle of the room, a raised octagonal pulpit surrounded by wooden rails holds stacks of well-worn prayer books with broken bindings. Long strips of plaster hang from the thirty-foot-high ceiling, which seems near collapse.

Tarnished plaques on the synagogue walls honor the Ashkenazic Jews from Romania, Poland, and Lithuania who founded this synagogue on Martins Junior Street in the late 1920s and maintained it over nearly seven decades. One written in Portuguese recognizes Bernard Schvartz, who funded a building renovation decades ago. Another plaque, written entirely in Hebrew, proudly cites the gift of another donor, who contributed 2 million in a long-lost Brazilian currency. Rows of dark wooden chairs bolted together are lined up to face the ark and are scattered at odd angles along the walls. Nearly every chair has a nameplate honoring an early member of the synagogue—Mesel, Kirzner, Schvartz, Auerbach, Katz, Rissin, Ribenboim. Yet on this Sabbath morning in late December, the names of most of the young men and women praying here—such as Braga, Oliveira, and Lopes—connote different origins. They are Recife's Marranos, descendants of Spanish and Portuguese refugees who were exiled more than 500 years ago and who preserved their practices under threats of persecution and death. Many continued their clandestine practices long after the danger had passed.

As the Torah service begins, Isaac Essoudry, the white-haired spiritual leader of this congregation, carries the large Torah scroll to the pulpit in the middle of the sanctuary. He sets it down on a long table, rolls it open to the weekly portion, touches the parchment with the fringes of his prayer shawl, and then kisses the fringes. Then he quickly rolls it closed. Although he is a skilled Torah reader, Essoudry instead reads the portion from a book in front of him, a *chummash* that contains the same biblical passages as the Torah.

The members of Essoudry's congregation have embraced Judaism, yet most Jews have not yet embraced the members. Visiting rabbis have ruled that these formerly secret Jews cannot be counted for a *minyan*, the ten Jewish men required to be present when the Torah is read. Essoudry can take the Torah from the ark, but under Jewish law, he cannot read from it.

The weekly portion is *Vayiggash*, the passage in which Joseph identifies himself to his brothers and sends them back to Canaan to bring their father, Jacob, and their families to Egypt. Before leaving Canaan, Jacob offers a sacrifice. God speaks to him:

And God spoke unto Israel in the visions of the night, and said: "Jacob, Jacob." And he said: "Here am I." And He said: "I am God, the God of they father; fear not to go down into Egypt; for I will there make of thee a great nation."

In recent years, some descendants of that great nation now living in Latin America, Spain, Portugal, New Mexico, and the Philippines have been rediscovering their hidden or lost Jewish roots. A few, like those in Recife and Belmonte, Portugal, are worshiping in the open for the first time in more than five centuries, and they wish to be accepted as Jews. These formerly secret Jews pose both an opportunity and a dilemma for world Jewry. They could help replenish and renew Jewish life in places where it has been weakened by assimilation and intermarriage. In Brazil alone there may be as many as 15 million people—more than the entire world Jewish population—who descend from Iberian Jewish exiles. Yet most rabbis will not accept them as Jews without formal conversion. And other Jewish communities, like the remaining descendants of Ashkenazic, or Eastern European, Jews in Recife, have shunned the Marranos.

ODMAR PINHEIRO BRAGA, a Recife police officer, philosophy student, and poet, is president of B'nai Anusim (Children of the Coerced), the religious congregation of Recife's secret Jews. He is tall and heavyset, with dark brown skin, a scraggly beard, and a large chip missing from one of his front teeth. He meets me for dinner and a late-night walk along Recife's beachfront wearing a gray Kangol-style hat, white shirt, and khaki pants with suspenders.

Many descendants of the Iberian Jewish exiles who were forced to convert to Christianity in the fifteenth and sixteenth centuries are unaware of their Jewish origins, Braga explains. But the Marranos—he uses this term with pride, despite its derisive connotation as the Spanish word for swine—have maintained their own culture and language within a closed circle for hundreds of years.

"No one is able to recognize a Marrano except another Marrano," Braga says between sips of milk from a coconut he bought from a vendor near the beach. "Our customs have not been lost, as many authors believe and try to make others believe."

Braga and other members of his congregation have remained Jews, he says, despite the doubts of Ashkenazic Jews about their origins and the questions raised by rabbis about marriages and divorces that may not have conformed to Jewish law. Braga insists there is no reason for them to convert to Judaism because they already are Jews.

"Can you turn salt into salt?" he asks.

Those who still consider themselves Marranos have sustained a different form of Judaism. Can they preserve it and still be considered Jews? Or must they abandon all practices and ways of thinking that do not conform to what Orthodox rabbis and the Askenazis in Recife define as traditional Judaism?

ODMAR BRAGA WAS born in Recife in the early 1950s. His parents were from northeastern Brazil—his mother from Paraíba, and his father from Mossoró. They both were secret Jews. Odmar was baptized as an infant, but not in a conventional Catholic church. Many of the secret Jews in Recife worshiped in a parish that had hired a Marrano to serve as a priest. The priest performed baptisms and heard confessions, but the secret Jews didn't take these practices seriously. They saw them as mock rituals to placate the church.

In his public school, Odmar says, all children were required to recite prayers each day. When the prayers required him to profess belief in Jesus and Mary, he crossed his fingers beneath his desk as a sign that he was lying. Once, he was almost expelled from school when he tore up a friend's saint cards and challenged the saints to curse him. Members of Odmar's family didn't work on the Jewish Sabbath and, like other secret Jews, lit candles clandestinely on Fridays at sunset, with the doors and curtains closed. His father read passages from the Hebrew Bible.

They kept other Jewish holidays as well, fasting on Yom Kippur and on the ninth of the Jewish month of Av to commemorate the destruction of the ancient Temples in Jerusalem. They ate a type of bitter herb on Passover, which they celebrated the week of Easter. His family never ate pork or shellfish, and they slaughtered chickens in a manner following the dictates of Jewish law—his mother cut the chicken's neck with a sharp knife, drained the blood, and soaked the meat in cold water.

Many of their other prayers and practices were unique to secret Jews. Odmar's family attached a portion from Psalm 91 to the back of their front door and recited lines from it on special occasions. They said a prayer to heal wounds, and they blessed children before they went to sleep so they wouldn't have bad dreams. When Odmar did have a nightmare, he would turn to a wall and repeat the bad dream so it wouldn't materialize. When they saw their enemies, secret Jews recited, "May God keep me away from the evil tongue, the evil eye, and the evil person I meet on the street"; and when they entered a church, said, "I don't go into this house to worship stone or wood, I worship the Eternal." Some of these traditions still are practiced today, Odmar says.

MARRANOS BELIEVE THEY descend from Jews who settled in Spain as early as the first century. In 616 C.E. the Visigoths converted to Catholicism and persecuted the Jews, ordering them to convert or leave Spain. The Jews later thrived under Arab rule, beginning in the eighth century. Many of them worked as tanners and textile makers and were famous throughout the world as gold- and silversmiths. The community also produced noted scholars, scientists, and political leaders. In the tenth and eleventh centuries, Muslim Spain was the source of great Jewish literature, philosophy, and science, much of it influenced by Arab culture. Ladino, a mixture of Spanish, Hebrew, Arabic, and several other languages, became the dialect of Spanish Jews. During the Middle Ages, Spain's Talmudic academies were the world's foremost centers of Jewish learning.

Tolerance for Jews diminished as the Christians reconquered Arab territories, culminating with a major Arab defeat in 1212. Initially, Jews remained relatively safe under Christian rule, despite laws limiting their participation in public life. After Jewish communities elsewhere in Europe were attacked and Jews were expelled from England, France, and much of Germany, virulent anti-Semitism took hold in Spain. In June 1391, inspired by religious zealots, Christians invaded the Jewish quarters of Seville and slaughtered 4,000 Jews. A wave of massacres spread throughout Spain later that year; Jewish communities in Córdoba, Toledo, Barcelona, and dozens of other towns and cities were wiped out and an estimated 50,000 Jews were killed. Hundreds of thousands more were forced to convert to Christianity.

Those who converted were called New Christians. They flourished in their new status in Spanish society and dominated professions from which they once had been banned. Many wealthy Jewish converts intermarried with Spanish nobility; middle-class Jewish converts became prominent lawyers, university professors, bankers, judges, and even bishops and priests. Most of the converts readily assimilated into Spanish society. Others, however, remained loyal to Judaism and observed Jewish practices in their homes.

Resentment against the success of the New Christians led to a new wave of attacks and massacres in the 1460s and 1470s and the expulsion of New Christians from many cities. In 1481, the Catholic church authorized an Inquisition in Spain to prosecute Marranos—in recent times also known as crypto Jews, *anusim,* or *conversos*—the converts who were charged with secretly practicing Judaism. Witnesses against them, threatened with torture or rewarded with bribes, accused them of remaining loyal to Judaism. Some scholars have argued that most of the charges were fabricated to sanction the confiscation of wealth and property and to justify the existence of the Inquisition. Thousands of Marranos were imprisoned, tortured, and, in some cases, burned at the stake. The relatively small number of Jews who had refused to convert were, for the most part, left alone.

In 1492, Spain's Edict of Expulsion required all remaining Jews to convert or emigrate. Many fled to North Africa, Italy, the Balkans, the Middle East, and Turkey. An estimated 300,000 Jews and Marranos escaped to neighboring Portugal, where Jews had thrived and enjoyed religious freedom. But in 1497, after the marriage of Spanish and Portuguese royalty, the Portuguese began their own forced conversions. These were far more brutal and widespread than in Spain. On the first day of Passover in 1497, one-fifth of Portugal's Jews were forcibly baptized and converted. Jewish children from families that resisted conversion were kidnapped, baptized, and taken away from their parents.

In Portugal, as in Spain, those who converted became prominent members of society. They excelled in banking, politics, economics, mathematics, medicine, and the arts. New Christians virtually monopolized the export business. And as in Spain, some even became members of the Catholic clergy. Yet most Jews who had undergone forced conversions continued to practice Judaism in secret.

Marranism was far more fervent and widespread in Portugal than it was in Spain. Women served as the spiritual leaders of the Marrano communities and passed down rituals. Fearing that their offspring would disclose the family's secret, they often waited until children were adolescents to inform them of their heritage. The women lit candles on Friday nights in their cellars or inside pitchers, and led prayers for Passover, Yom Kippur, and the Fast of Esther. The Marranos often celebrated holidays a day or two later than the fixed dates to help keep their practices hidden in case a priest or neighbor visited during the holidays.

Persecution against the Jews in Portugal continued throughout the sixteenth century. In 1506, more than 2,000 New Christians were massacred in Lisbon. By 1539, a Court of Inquisition had begun to prosecute New Christians. When emigration laws were occasionally relaxed, tens of thousands of Jews left the country; many joined Spanish exiles in southern Europe, North Africa, and the Middle East. Others escaped to the Americas, where secret Jews had accompanied Christopher Columbus, who himself may have been a secret Jew. Portugal also began to deport criminals and so-called Judaizers to its colony in Brazil. An estimated one in every ten settlers of Brazil was a Marrano.

Many became practicing Catholics and lost touch with their past; others returned to Judaism. The terror of the Inquisition, however, soon reached Brazil. In 1580, the Catholic church authorized the bishop in Bahia to investigate accusations against secret Jews and send suspects to Lisbon for imprisonment and trial. A brief era of religious freedom flowered in northeastern Brazil after the Dutch conquered it in 1630. Marranos joyously greeted the Dutch soldiers. Portugal then accused the Marranos of collaborating in the Dutch victory.

The Dutch held the northeast coastal cities for nearly twenty-five years. They established Dutch Reform churches and tolerated other religious beliefs. Marranos from other parts of Brazil moved to Recife, Olinda, and other towns in the region and practiced Judaism openly. In 1636, they founded the first synagogue in the Americas, Tsur Israel (Rock of Israel). The street on which it was located was named Street of the Jews. In 1641, 200 Jewish settlers from Amsterdam arrived in Recife with Rabbi Isaac Aboab and practiced together with the Marranos. Several other synagogues were established in surrounding towns in the 1640s.

In 1654, the Portuguese reconquered the northeast. In Re-cife, Street of the Jews was renamed Street of the Cross. (It is now called Benevolent Jesus Street.) The synagogue site was commemorated by a plaque on a wall behind an outdoor café.

Most of the Dutch Jews emigrated—150 Jewish families re-turned to Amsterdam—and the synagogues were closed. Some Brazilian Marranos also left and dispersed throughout the New World, establishing Jewish communities in places like Jamaica, Barbados, and Surinam. Twenty-three Marrano refugees from Brazil founded a Jewish community in New York and estab-lished the Shearith Israel synagogue, still an active congregation today at Central Park West and West 70th Street.

For the Marranos who remained in Brazil, the Inquisition re-turned with a vengeance after the defeat of the Dutch. Church authorities hunted down and persecuted secret Jews, charging them with observing the Sabbath and other Jewish holidays, kosher slaughter, circumcision, and Jewish burial practices. Over the next two centuries, 400 Marranos from Brazil were sent to Lisbon on charges that they were secretly practicing Judaism. Eighteen of them were condemned to death, including one who was burned alive after refusing to renounce his Judaism.

There were fewer persecutions in the northeast, which is somewhat isolated from the rest of Brazil. Yet more than half of the population descended from secret Jews and many of the Marranos continued their ceremonies, establishing secret syna-gogues, worshiping with their own rabbis, and perhaps even reading from Torah scrolls they had preserved.

The last execution of a Brazilian Marrano took place in 1769; laws discriminating against New Christians were revoked in 1773. Jews who openly professed their religion began to arrive in Brazil after 1822, when the nation declared its independence from Portugal.

Inquisition records provide detailed documentation that secret Jewish practices survived through the hundreds of years of persecution. Arnold Wiznitzer, in *Jews in Colonial Brazil,* writes that the Marranos gradually assimilated into Catholicism. David M. Gitlitz, in *Secrecy and Deceit,* concludes that Marranism disappeared in the Americas soon after the Inquisition was disbanded. Yet there is other evidence, much of it anecdotal, that Marranism continued even after the persecutions stopped.

In the 1960s and 1970s, sociologists reported that some Mexicans believe they descend from Jews. Scholars also found that secret Jewish practices had survived among descendants of Marranos in the American Southwest. Rabbis in New Mexico told sociologist Schulamith C. Halevy that they had met privately with Spanish-speaking men and women who believe their ancestors were Sephardic Jews. A rabbi who had served in Albuquerque for thirty years said he had spoken with several dozen local people who described secret Jewish traditions passed down by older Hispanic women. Halevy also interviewed hundreds of Hispanics in the Azores, Mallorca, Canada, the Philippines, and throughout Central and South America and the United States who know or suspect that they descend from Jews. Some of them, Halevy writes, continue to follow customs that can be traced to Sephardic Jewry.

Marrano practices are perhaps most widespread in Brazil. As a student at Hebrew Union College in Cincinnati, Rabbi

Jacques Cukierkorn, who was raised in São Paulo, documented some of the traditions still common among descendants of secret Jews. In Venhaver, an isolated village of about 1,400 people in the mountains of northeastern Brazil, Cukierkorn found people with light skin and blue eyes who followed their own versions of Jewish practice.

The people of Venhaver are, on the surface, Catholics. They attend church regularly, although they refuse to kneel. They keep images of saints and crosses in their homes, yet the transverse piece of the cross is often at an odd angle. The villagers also follow many Jewish practices. They do not eat pork, or fish without scales and fins, and they do not mix milk with meat. They slaughter chickens in a manner similar to the requirements of Jewish law. On Friday nights, the women light two candles but keep them away from the windows. They refuse to eat bread during the first week of April, approximating the Jewish Festival of Passover. Burial follows Jewish rather than Christian ritual, including wrapping the corpse in a linen shroud. The burial is followed by a seven-day period of mourning. Family members often leave pebbles on graves, sometimes in the shape of a Star of David.

Yet Anita Novinsky, a professor of history at the University of São Paolo, suggests that many of those who claim to be Marranos and practice secret Jewish rituals descend from Christians who adopted Jewish traditions, not from forced converts who fled Spain and Portugal. The picture has been clouded further by widespread publicity about the emergence of *anusim* and a resurgence of interest in researching family lineages. Some purported secret Jews have boasted about inventing their history after entertaining gullible journalists and researchers with their stories.

Halevy argues, however, that many Marrano practices in the Americas today could not have been learned by Christians who became secret Jews. She found, for example, that it was common among Marrano women—usually older women—to clean their houses by sweeping to the middle of a room. The origin of this is obscure, but it was widespread among Jews in ancient Spain. A seventeenth-century commentary suggests it may have been done to keep dust away from the *mezuzah*. Under the Inquisition, women were incriminated as secret Jews for cleaning their houses in this way.

Some scholars believe that other Marrano traditions, such as lighting candles on Friday nights and burying the dead in linen shrouds, easily could have been learned from other Jews. But some families can trace these rituals back for many generations; except for the brief period of Dutch rule in northeastern Brazil in the seventeenth century, Judaism was not professed openly in Latin America until the 1820s. The first Ashkenazic Jews didn't arrive until the late 1800s. Halevy also dismisses suggestions that secret Jews could have learned about these rituals from Inquisition records.

"It would have been foolhardy for an 'old' Christian or sincere convert to maintain any practice, however, trivial" that could have led to his imprisonment or death, Halevy writes. "Only *anusim* [coerced ones] with heroic interest in preserving their heritage would risk their well-being and that of their families for the sake of a forbidden tradition."

WHEN ODMAR WAS twelve years old, he attended Sabbath services at the synagogue on Martins Junior Street with
his aunt. His aunt, like several other older Marranas, often
went to Sabbath services and sat quietly in the balcony, keeping her distance from the Ashkenazic women who occasionally
glared in her direction. Odmar was overwhelmed by the mysterious Hebrew words and Jewish rituals, he recalls; it was as
if he had connected with his past for the first time.

In the following months, Odmar regularly attended services
on the Sabbath and the Jewish holidays and sat among the male
congregants. Most of the Ashkenazis were unfriendly, but a
few of the older men helped him follow the service and taught
him some of the prayers.

Odmar's study of Judaism was interrupted by his military
service. Other than his baptism, Odmar says, the only other
time he performed a Catholic ritual was when his captain in the
army, a priest, told him to he had to take communion at Easter.

"Are you talking to me as a priest or as a captain?" Odmar
had asked him.

"As a priest."

"Then I prefer not to do it," Odmar had replied.

"Then as a captain, I order you. If you refuse, I'll have you
sent to jail."

Odmar relented. The captain had Odmar's picture taken
during communion to further humiliate him. Odmar still keeps
a copy of that photograph.

While he was in the army, Odmar married his childhood

sweetheart, Maria das Graças, also from a Marrano family. It was a civil ceremony, but Odmar and Maria vowed to establish a Jewish home. When he returned to civilian life, Odmar found work in Recife as a beat cop. He also began to study at night for a master's degree in philosophy at a local university. Odmar later was promoted to supervise the administrative division for the regional police. Three other members of his division are Marranos. Police in Brazil are poorly paid, routinely corrupt, and generally mistrusted. For Marranos, however, jobs related to law enforcement—police, attorneys, and judges—offer opportunities for them to help protect themselves.

Odmar and his wife have three children, two girls and a boy, and are raising them as Jews. The oldest, Hoseanna, is married and has an infant daughter, Sarah. Their second daughter, Osineide, is a teenager and attends public school. One of her teachers knows Odmar and once told the class that they should be proud to attend school with a Marrana, a descendant of the first Jews to arrive in Brazil. But many of Osineide's Christian classmates stopped talking to her. Odmar and Maria's youngest child, a boy named Obadiah, was born with a heart condition and wasn't circumcised, but Odmar says he is now healthy enough for a ritual circumcision. Obadiah also has encountered some discrimination in school, but for being a Jew, not a Marrano. Obadiah has inherited his father's quick wit and strong will. When he was told to sing *Ave Maria* in public school, he instead sang the *Shema,* the sacred prayer affirming a belief in one God that Jews have recited for thousands of years.

Odmar hopes to enroll his children in the Jewish day school

run by the Ashkenazic community; Osineide recently passed the entrance examination. Odmar hasn't yet figured out how to pay for it, since the tuition is far more than he can afford. But he is being pressured by some of the secret Jews not to send her. They feel that sending her to school with the Ashkenazis would betray the Marranos.

At home, the family celebrates a traditional Jewish Sabbath. On Fridays, Maria cleans the house, makes *challah,* and prepares the Sabbath meal. Like many other Jews, she lights the Sabbath candles at sunset near a window facing the street, and recites the Hebrew prayer, abandoning the Marrana practice of hiding the candles from view. Then Odmar blesses the children, first in the secret tradition—each child asks for a blessing, kisses Odmar's hand, and Odmar recites, "May the Eternal bless you and keep you"—and then in the traditional Jewish one—Odmar says, "May God make you like Ephraim and Manasseh," to his son, and "May God make you like Sarah, Rebecca, Rachel, and Leah" to his daughters and granddaughter.

Neither Odmar nor Maria works on the Sabbath, and they both follow the Orthodox rules that prohibit turning on or off lights and appliances. Odmar does violate one Orthodox mandate by driving to services, since they live a great distance from the synagogue.

"There are six hundred thirteen *mitzvot* (commandments)," Odmar says. "It's better to follow six hundred than none."

IN THE EARLY 1980s, Odmar and others who had been attending services at the Martins Junior synagogue founded a

Marrano group called Gates of Redemption. Over the next decade, dozens of Marranos set aside their fears and obsession for secrecy and together celebrated the Sabbath and Jewish holidays at the synagogue.

Although he is a Sephardic Jew, Isaac Essoudry had been the spiritual leader of the Ashkenazic congregation since 1975. At first he barely acknowledged Odmar and the other Marranos. The older members of the congregation would question them at the door and ask them to sit at some distance from the regular congregants. On the High Holidays, the Ashkenazis barred the Marranos from attending services. Essoudry refused to instruct them during his classes after Sabbath services. He told them they would have to convert before he would teach them about the Torah and the Hebrew prayers. Nonetheless, they sat in on his classes and learned the prayers on their own.

A descendant of devout Moroccan Jews, Essoudry was born in Belém in 1935. He grew up with his family in Morocco and Israel, then returned to Belém to marry when he was twenty-one. He moved to Recife in 1962 and has been a member of the synagogue on Martins Junior Street ever since.

Essoudry had struggled to make a living as a taxi driver and from the small salary he received from the congregation as its leader and head of the burial society. His wife, a fellow Moroccan Sephardi, was unhappy with their standard of living, he says, and divorced him for that reason in 1979. He remarried in 1981, to a Marrana. They have three children, two boys and a girl.

Eventually, Essoudry was so impressed by the Marranos' devotion and persistence that he became their champion and teacher. He convinced the Ashkenazis to let them enter the synagogue and participate in study classes.

"I don't care who's a Marrano or who's not," Essoudry says. "In my opinion, they are of Jewish descent and were cut off. There is a lapse in the continuity of their Judaism. Today they are remembering that they are Jewish and have Jewish blood."

Among Essoudry's new students were Luciano Lopes and Heloisa Fonseca. Lopes, a tall, thin man who works as a graphic designer, is intensely religious—he is one of the members of the congregation who has grown side curls—and hopes to study in a *yeshiva* and become a rabbi. Lopes grew up in São Paulo. Both of his parents descended from Marranos, and they continued their secret practices as he was growing up. On Friday nights, his mother would close the doors and curtains at home and light candles, offering a silent prayer, she would tell him, "to the angels." In school, the Catholic children taunted him and other Marranos—they called them billy goats—because they followed unusual beliefs and didn't go to church. The Marranos kept to themselves.

For as long as he can remember, Lopes's father told him that he was different, that he was descended from Jews. His family moved to Recife, and when he was nineteen, Lopes visited a synagogue for the first time, the one on Martins Junior Street. He was entranced by the sounds of the Hebrew prayers. Lopes began to study Torah and the Talmud, the ancient rabbinic commentaries on Jewish law. After less than five years, he can read and speak Hebrew fluently, is well versed in the Torah, and can read and understand obscure Talmudic commentary in both Hebrew and Aramaic.

Heloisa Fonseca, a cheerful woman in her forties, grew up in Recife. She knew her family was different from the Catholics with whom she grew up; her parents never ate pork or shell-fish, and on Friday nights they lit candles and blessed the children. When her grandfather was about to die, he said he heard the voices of his dead relatives calling to him, a common tale among Marrano families. His funeral followed Jewish practice: They washed his body, wrapped it in a linen shroud, placed him in a coffin, and buried him the next day, his feet facing east toward Jerusalem. During the weeklong mourning period, Fonseca's family covered all their windows and mirrors with black cloth.

Her parents didn't tell her she was descended from Jews until she was nineteen. She later married a Navy veteran from the United States named Joseph Fonseca, who also descended from Marranos. When Heloisa first came to the synagogue on Martins Junior Street twenty years ago, a few Ashkenazic women in the balcony confronted her and asked her what she was doing there, but she knew she belonged.

BY THE EARLY 1990s, the Marranos made up a majority of the congregation at the Martins Junior Street synagogue. Most Ashkenazic families had moved to Boa Viagem and to other upscale neighborhoods along the beachfront, and had virtually abandoned their original synagogue. The old center of Recife didn't seem safe to many of them, and there was no place to park.

There are now about 1,500 Ashkenzic Jews in Recife,

Brazil's fourth-largest city with a population of 1.5 million. The numbers are difficult to estimate because the intermarriage rate among Ashkenazis in Recife is nearly 90 percent. A new liberal reform group, made up mostly of intermarried couples, holds services on Friday nights at the Jewish community center, the Centro Israelita de Pernambuco, on the outskirts of the city. The handful who regularly attend services on Saturday worship with the only rabbi in town, a Lubavitcher from Belém who runs a synagogue near a shopping mall. The rabbi, Joseph ben Zeckry, has welcomed one Marrano to his congregation.

"That one is a true Marrano," the rabbi says to me from behind the wheel of his minivan as he prepares to leave on a field trip with two visiting Americans. "The others who came here aren't true Marranos; they don't have genealogical proof. There could be people in their families who married gentiles or who weren't properly divorced. A few of them came here for a few months to study and thought they had learned everything, but they know very little. They're welcome to come back to study, but they will have to convert to Judaism."

IN 1995, THE Marranos who attended services at the Martins Junior synagogue decided to form their own congregation. Odmar says many other Marranos urged them to remain in hiding and maintain their old traditions and practices. Odmar disagreed. "To live Judaism," he says, "we had to abandon the Marrano way."

Before they did so, however, they sought the approval of a mysterious brotherhood known as the *custodio*. Odmar says that *custodios* throughout the country have protected the Marranos since they first settled in Brazil. They are headed by secret Jews who have kept their identities hidden.

The head of Recife's *custodio,* who asked me not to identify him by name, works in an anonymous office building in down-town Recife. When Odmar and I arrive after business hours, the long hallway to the office is unlit and an iron gate protects the front door. The head of the *custodio* unlocks the gate and greets us. His steely good looks and confidence are reminiscent of Al Pacino's in *The Godfather.* He speaks in a formal, some-what stilted English. He invites us inside his book-lined suite, furnished with black leather chairs and couches, and introduces his wife, who serves us espresso from a small machine on a table near his desk. He shows us books of letters and diaries from family members who lived as secret Jews in Brazil for hundreds of years.

"We understand that man is evil by nature and always will be capable of evil," he says. "Nothing has changed. Even though we respect and support what Odmar's congregation has done, we know we must continue to remain secret and to be here to protect one another."

There are rumors that the *custodios* have assassinated people who have threatened the Marranos. I ask if this still occurs.

"Oh, no," he says with a broad smile. "We haven't done that for at least ten years."

Odmar later explains that many Marranos fear that forming a congregation will lead to further harassment. Schulamith Halevy has noted that several secret Jews, especially in Mexico, have been murdered in recent years, although there is no firm proof they were killed because of their beliefs. Those who have openly returned to Judaism have received hate mail and have been harassed by Christian missionaries. They also face mistrust and prejudice from the Jewish community.

"We never proposed an integration with the rest of the Jewish community," Odmar says. "We never asked for anything. We came to the Ashkenazic synagogue to worship in the open, to breathe. But we can always retreat. If the Jewish world is not ready to accept us, we'll go back into hiding."

The Marranos renamed their group the Sephardic Religious B'nai Anusim, and elected Odmar president. They added Sephardic prayers and songs in Ladino to the services at the Martins Junior synagogue.

A few of the Ashkenazis still come there on Saturdays, usually for a special occasion, such as a *bar* or *bat mitzvah,* a circumcision, or a baby naming. Dozens more come for the High Holidays and seem comfortable praying with the Marranos. At the close of services on a recent Yom Kippur, the Marranos spontaneously sang a Ladino version of a song celebrating the end of the Sabbath; the Ashkenazis at the service broke into enthusiastic applause. Essoudry took that as a sign that the Marranos are being accepted. "I don't think so," Odmar tells me later. "Probably they applauded because we sang well."

ONE SATURDAY IN October 1996, a year after B'nai Anusim was established, a group of visiting American and Canadian Jews joined the Marranos in celebrating the Sabbath at the Martins Junior synagogue. One of the visitors, Irwin M. Berg, a New York attorney, was so moved by their sincerity and devotion to Judaism that he offered to assist them in their efforts to be recognized as Jews.

Odmar, his congregants, and other Marranos in the northeast considered Berg's offer and decided he could help them. After lengthy discussions, they agreed to ask Berg to write a letter to Rabbi Joseph Sebag, a Sephardic rabbi from Israel who had assisted about 200 secret Jews in Belmonte, a small Portuguese community in the mountains near the Spanish border. The community was first discovered in 1917 when M. Samuel Schwarz, a Polish-born mining engineer from Lisbon, found hundreds of Marranos who observed the Sabbath and several Jewish holidays, secretly lit candles on Friday nights, rejected belief in Jesus and the saints, and married only among themselves. They knew only one word in Hebrew—*Adonai*, the word for God. In the following years, Schwarz and others discovered similar small communities of Marranos in other northern villages. More than seventy years later, the Belmonte Marranos voted to openly embrace Judaism. With Rabbi Sebag's help, they studied modern Jewish practices and underwent circumcisions, immersions in a ritual bath, and formal conversions, returning to Judaism after 500 years of worshiping in secret.

In his letter, Berg described what he had seen during his Sabbath visit to Recife, and urged Sebag to assist and perhaps visit the congregation.

The B'nai Anusim of Recife say that they have preserved the traditions of their parents over the centuries under difficult and oftentimes dangerous conditions. They are proud of their Sephardic roots. . . . They are the remnants *(Shearith Yisrael)* of millions who descend from the Portuguese *conversos* and Marranos of Brazil. Largely, by their own efforts, they are teaching themselves the *mitzvoth, halachoth, minghagim* [commandments, laws, customs], and the prayers and ceremonies of Judaism.

In my opinion, the three greatest disasters in Jewish history were the destruction of the Temple in 70 C.E., the expulsion and forcible conversion of the Jews of the Iberian Peninsula at the end of the 15th century, and the Holocaust in our time. After the first disaster, the Jewish spark was preserved at Yavneh [a center of learning in ancient Israel], and after the third disaster the Jewish spark was lit in *Eretz Yisrael* [the Land of Israel]. We are now witnessing the rekindling of the Jewish spark among the descendants of the second of these disasters. It is an event of momentous, historic proportions.

Sebag replied several weeks later that he was eager to help the community and to visit them, but was doubtful they could afford to pay his expenses. In May, Odmar organized a B'nai Anusim poetry show and national conference. It was held in the auditorium at police headquarters.

At the conference, representatives from Recife, Fortaleza, Natal, Goiânia, and other cities and towns came to discuss religious practices, Rabbi Sebag's proposed visit, and the formation of a B'nai Anusim council, which elected Odmar as their first national president. They decided that Sebag should visit several towns and that the costs of his visit should be divided among all of the represented Marrano communities.

A few communities made small contributions, but Odmar raised most of the money, about $6,000, on his own. Sebag arrived in August 1997 for a two-week tour of Marrano communities in Brazil.

"He spoke to many people," Odmar tells me, "and he asked about our traditions. He even went with us into the interior [in northeastern Brazil] to meet with Marranos who have lineage dating back to the seventeenth century. He wanted to know everything, even the way we slaughter animals. So we showed him how we do it; he said it was no different than the traditional Sephardic way."

Sebag told Odmar he believes that the Recife Marranos are an emerging Jewish community. He uttered the words Odmar and his fellow congregants wanted to hear. "He said we should engage in a process of return, not conversion," Odmar says.

"I told Rabbi Sebag that I would rather die a Marrano than convert to anything," Odmar says. "He told me, 'That's exactly what it means to be a Marrano.'"

Under Jewish law, Jews who convert to another faith are still considered Jews. After Jews were forcibly converted in Spain as early as the twelfth century, the great scholar Moses Maimonides wrote that Jews who had been coerced yet secretly followed some commandments should be welcomed and encouraged to practice as Jews, not shunned. In the fifteenth century, Rabbi Solomon ben Simeon Duran composed a prayer for forced converts who wanted to return to Judaism: "Our God and God of our fathers, bring success to Your servant . . . and bestow Your grace upon him. Just as You have moved his heart to return in complete repentance before You, so may You plant in his heart love and fear of You. . . ."

Most rabbis require Marranos to convert to Judaism if they wish to be accepted as Jews unless they can prove, with genealogical records, that they descended from Jews. Others, including Mordechai Eliahu, the former chief rabbi of Israel, advocate reviving the "return" ceremony for secret Jews. It is similar to conversion—it includes requirements for circumcision and immersion—as well as Rabbi Duran's prayer. Those who complete the ceremony receive a certificate of return rather than of conversion.

Rabbi Sebag recommended that the Marranos continue to study and follow Jewish law, and offered to send Ya'acov de Oliveira, a young man originally from the center of Brazil who was trained at a *yeshiva* in Israel, to work with them. As soon as the rabbi left, Odmar began to raise money again, this time to provide Oliveira with a home and living expenses. Odmar says he expects that the young man will teach and advise the Marranos as well as perform ceremonies. Yet he remains typically cautious.

"He will not be here to conduct a sort of ideological patrol," Odmar says. "But he has to be loyal to Sebag while he is serving us. We will observe him very carefully and see what happens."

Most leaders of the Ashkenazic community still do not consider the Marranos Jews. Some say privately that the Marranos are defiling the Torah by removing it from the ark without the presence of ten Jewish men. Their antagonism to the Marranos mirrors the often ridiculed contentiousness among different forms of Judaism.

"The issue needs to be studied," Dr. Boris Berenstein, head of the Recife Jewish Federation, tells me in a telephone interview. "The board is talking and we need to talk with the Marranos. We need to give Isaac [Essoudry] some guidelines, some limits."

Marcelo Kosminski, another Federation board member, says the Marranos haven't tried to work with the Ashkenazic community.

"They're predisposed to thinking they won't be accepted," he tells me between calls on his cellular phone as he sits beside the pool at the Jewish community center while his children swim. He says he believes the Ashkenazis will close the old synagogue and turn it into a museum or a cultural center. His wife, Beatrice, sitting next to him, seems more sympathetic.

"The Marranos have lots of feeling for Judaism, even more than traditional Jews," Mrs. Kosminski says. "They really want to be Jewish. And we Jews need to add, not diminish, our numbers."

She believes, however, that the Marranos will have to convert and show that they can integrate themselves to be accepted. "Anyone can say they're a Marrano," she says.

Odmar believes that the main issue for the future of the Jewish community is not the Marrano question.

"We are the strong flame," Odmar says. "The problem is with the flame that is dying out, the Ashkenazis. We would like to help them survive.

"The best way would be for all Jews to get along and pray in one synagogue," he says. "But the Ashkenazis want to deny our existence; we don't negate theirs. Some Ashkenazis say that even if the rabbis recognize you as Jews, we won't accept you. They'd rather have their children marry a non-Jew than a Marrano. It all comes down to the issue of money. If the Marranos had money, they'd be accepted. No one wants to marry a poor person."

ISAAC ESSOUDRY'S WEEKLY study class begins after the Torah service and a kosher lunch. About once a month, some Marrano students from Natal and Fortaleza, more than 400 miles from Recife, come here for class. The early January day I attend, the discussion focuses on the following week's Torah portion, the story of Jacob's blessing of his grandsons and his testament and death. The passage is the source of the mysterious blessing that many Jewish families recite to their sons on Friday nights: "May God make you like Ephraim and Manasseh."

Idelmar Rodrigues, a tall, tough-looking cop in his mid-thirties with short, dark hair and long sideburns, joins in the discussion. Rodrigues is married to a Japanese woman, a descendant of shoguns, and they have two boys and two girls; he is one of the few Marranos in the congregation who has married a non-Marrano.

"Joseph married a non-Jew," Rodrigues says, raising his voice, "yet his children were considered Jewish and were blessed by his father, Jacob. Ephraim and Manasseh are the models for all Jewish children. So why are my children not considered Jews?"

A visiting rabbi explains that for Conservative and Orthodox rabbis, a person isn't a Jew unless he can establish that he descends from a line of Jewish mothers or has formally converted to Judaism. (Some Reform rabbis now recognize both patrilineal and matrilineal descent.) Rodrigues's children face the additional burden of having to document 500 years of uninterrupted Jewish genealogy, a nearly impossible task. Rodrigues doesn't seem satisfied with the rabbi's explanation.

After the Torah class, the congregants complete their prayers with the *Havdalah* service, signifying the end of the Sabbath. Essoudry lights the braided *Havdalah* candle, blesses the wine, and passes around the spices as the congregants join in welcoming Elijah the prophet and singing the Hebrew song *"Hamavdeel bein kodesh."* Odmar's deep bass and Heloisa Fonseca's splendid soprano echo through this fading sanctuary and back in time.

> *He who separates the sacred from the profane,*
> *May He pardon our sins,*
> *May He increase our descendants and prosperity*
> *As the sand and as the stars at night.*

Marranos believe they descend from Jews . . . many joined Spanish exiles in Southern Europe, North Africa, and the Middle East.   Cecil Roth, *A History of the Marranos,* 4th ed. (New York: Hermon Press, 1974), pp. 7–98.

Portugal also began to deport criminals and so-called Judaizers . . .

Ibid.; Arnold Wiznitzer, *Jews in Colonial Brazil* (New York: Columbia University Press, 1960), p. 12.

The Dutch held the northeast . . . including one who was burned alive after refusing to renounce his Judaism.   Roth, *A History of the Marranos;* Wiznitzer, *Jews in Colonial Brazil,* pp. 58, 60, 128–67.

There were fewer persecutions in the northeast . . .   Andrée Brooks, "Jewish Voyagers to the New World Emerging from History's Mists," *New York Times,* July 29, 1997, p. C4.

The last execution . . .   Wiznitzer, *Jews in Colonial Brazil.*

In the 1960s and 1970s . . .   Schulamith C. Halevy, "Manifestations of Crypto-Judaism in the American Southwest" <http://www-csgso.cs.edu/ ñachum/sch/sch/Folklore.txt>.

As a student at Hebrew Union College . . .   Jacques Cukierkorn, "Retornando—Coming Back" (Thesis, Hebrew Union College, Cincinnati, 1994).

Halevy argues, however . . . "for the sake of a forbidden tradition." Halevy, "Manifestations"; Halevy, "Obscure Practices Among New World Anusim" <http://www-csgso.cs.uiuc.edu/-nachum/sch/sch/Obscure.txt>.

The community was first discovered in 1917 . . . in other northern villages.   Roth, *A History of the Marranos,* pp. 363–76.

After Jews were forcibly converted . . . certificate of return rather than of conversion.   Schulamith C. Halevy, "Notes from a Friend on Conversion to Judaism" <http://www-csgso.cs.uiuc.edu/-nachum/sch/sch/conversion.html>.

Chapter Six

PEOPLE OF THE BOOK

I crouch down and drop to my knees on the soft brown-and-burgundy Persian carpet. Then, imitating the men around me, I stretch out my arms, lean forward, and rest my palms and forehead on the carpet as members of the congregation chant a prayer confessing their sins, lamenting the destruction of the ancient Temple in Jerusalem, and asking God for forgiveness.

Everything seems both familiar and strange. The sanctuary looks like other Jewish synagogues, with a high ceiling, tall windows, and a raised pulpit at one end. A long blue curtain covers the ark, with a maroon tapestry above it representing the Ten Commandments. Unlike other synagogues, however, this one in Ashdod, Israel, is sparsely furnished. There are only a handful of chairs at the back, where a few of the older men are seated. Dozens of small silver bowls, like ancient candleholders, hang about six feet above the floor from chains attached to the arched ceiling along both sides of the sanctuary. The only decorations on the walls are Hebrew phrases from the Torah.

The men and boys all wear skullcaps and prayer shawls, but unlike the shawls worn in other synagogues, these have one blue string hanging among the white strings on either end. It is also unusual to see men praying in stocking feet; they have removed their shoes and placed them on wooden shelves in an anteroom. There is a sink in the anteroom where congregants wash their hands before entering the sanctuary, a practice not followed in other synagogues.

I recognize many of the verses in the Hebrew prayer book, psalms beseeching God to accept our prayers. Yet it is odd to see Jews pray on their knees and bow; the only parallel is during the High Holidays, when most Orthodox Jews—and rabbis and cantors in Reform and Conservative synagogues—traditionally prostrate themselves before the ark and ask God to forgive their sins.

On this Saturday in Ashdod, on the Mediterranean coast south of Tel Aviv, I am praying with a congregation of Karaites, members of what is arguably the only surviving ancient Jewish sect. The Karaites consider themselves Jews but remain separate, and they follow customs not practiced by other Jews, whom they call Rabbanites. Karaites trace their spiritual origins to the early days of Judaism; many of their religious practices replicate customs followed by worshipers in the Temple in Jerusalem more than two millennia ago. They use the Bible as the source for most of their prayers and customs, rejecting rabbinical interpretations and oral law. Their name apparently derives from the Hebrew word for scriptures, *mikra;* they believe they are the true People of the Book.

At one time, Karaism was a major branch of Judaism and posed a serious challenge to the rabbis and their followers. Today, only a few thousand Karaites remain, mostly of Egyptian origin. Nearly all of them live in Israel. Orthodox rabbis have accepted them as Jews but have refused to recognize the authority of their religious leaders.

THE THREE-HOUR Sabbath service concludes at about 10:00 A.M., and Eliyahu Dabbach, a short, balding man in his mid-sixties, leads us from the synagogue to his apartment building five blocks away. We walk up one flight of stairs to his apartment. On this mid-August morning, it is stiflingly hot inside, with no fans or air conditioners running. Karaite doctrine forbids some practices followed by Orthodox Jews on the Sabbath, such as using automatic timers to turn on lights and air conditioners, and riding Sabbath elevators that are programmed to stop on every floor.

Eliyahu's wife, Nehama, invites us to sit at the dining room table for what she calls breakfast, since it is still mid-morning. The table is covered with a linen cloth, platters of vegetables, and several large blue thermoses. Before we begin eating, Eliyahu reads the customary Hebrew blessings. He holds the prayer book close to his thick, round glasses as he chants. Eliyahu has been legally blind for much of his adulthood.

Nehama, a solidly built woman with a gentle manner, then unscrews the top from one of the thermoses and pours a mixture of fava beans and hard-boiled eggs onto our plates. It is redolent with garlic, lemon, and black pepper. Egyptian Karaites like Nehama cook this Middle Eastern dish, called *ful,* the day before the Sabbath, and keep it warm in thermoses. Karaites believe that even keeping food warm in an oven after sunset, a practice followed by Orthodox Jews, violates biblical prohibitions against using a fire on the Sabbath. Afterward, we sit in the living room, where Nehama serves fruit, roasted seeds, and homemade pastries as she and Eliyahu talk with us.

Eliyahu was born in Cairo in 1933. Like many Egyptian Karaites, the Dabbachs were jewelers. They had been money-changers for several generations but switched to the jewelry business when banks took over lending late in the nineteenth century. The Dabbachs' specialty was gold and silver nose ornaments customarily worn by Egyptian women.

Nehama was born in 1943, also in Cairo. Her father was a textile peddler, and her mother a tailor. Other members of her family made currency for the British-run government, gold and silver coins with images of Queen Victoria and Arabic lettering.

Both Nehama and Eliyahu were born in the Karaite quarter, known as Harat al-Karrah, although they didn't meet until years later when they lived in Israel. Some of the narrow, unpaved lanes in the quarter were named for Karaite families. Eliyahu's family lived close to Atfit Dabbach, or Dabbach Lane. He was their firstborn child, and shortly after he was born, his aunt Latifa—his mother's older sister, a blind, unmarried woman who lived next door—adopted him. Latifa later adopted his firstborn sister as well. Eliyahu and his sister never questioned their mother's decision; such adoptions were common among childless Muslim and Karaite women in Egypt. Eliyahu's mother raised her two other children, her second son and second daughter.

Eliyahu attended government-run schools and went to services at a nearby Karaite synagogue. Like many Jews who grow up in the diaspora, he learned to read Hebrew but didn't understand it. He had just enough training to complete his *bar mitzvah* under the guidance of Tobiah Levi Babovitch, the *hacham*, or Karaite religious leader, in Cairo. Babovitch had been born in Russia and worked as a teacher in Karaite schools there. He had served as a *hacham* in the Crimea before he was named to the post in Cairo in 1934.

Babovitch was a published scholar who had written articles and books on Karaite history and religion. Although some leaders of the Karaite community supported intermarriage and closer relations with the Rabbanites, Babovitch upheld the ban on conversion to Karaism and adhered to the strict view that a Karaite who married a Rabbanite should be excluded from the Karaite community.

THERE IS WIDE disagreement among Karaites about their customs, practices, and even their history. Some Karaites believe their roots date back to the tenth century B.C.E., when Jewish leaders proclaimed that God had handed down two sets of laws on Mt. Sinai, the written law of the Torah and an oral law that Moses related to his people. Others believe Karaism

began in ancient Israel in the first century B.C.E. with the emergence of the Sadducees, Essenes, and other sects that opposed
the Pharisees and their use of oral law to interpret the Bible.
Some sects broke away to establish separate religions, including
the Samaritans (people who believe they descend from the
original inhabitants of Samaria and still follow biblical practices,
including animal sacrifice on Passover) and the Christians. The
Pharisees became the dominant movement in Judaism. Many
Karaites see themselves as heirs to the Sadducees, a dissenting
group that remained part of Judaism, although there is no documentary proof of an historic link.

Most historians conclude that Karaism first emerged much
later in Persia. Under Sassanid rule, beginning in the third century C.E., Persian Jews had become an autonomous community,
headed by an exilarch who represented them before the king,
collected taxes, and administered justice. Scholars in the rabbinic
academies were in charge of religion and legal theory; they ex-
plained and codified the laws of the Bible. By the seventh century, the academies had compiled the oral laws into the
Babylonian Talmud, a massive encyclopedia of debates, stories,
and lessons about Jewish history, law, and ethics. It was not only
a great literary achievement but also a spiritual guide that helped
Judaism survive through the centuries.

After the Arabs conquered Persia in the seventh century, the
new rulers maintained the system of Jewish autonomy as the
rabbinic academies grew in power and the authority of the exilarch declined. The academies, headed by a *gaon* (eminence),
spawned a large bureaucracy that approved laws and adjudicated
appeals. When the Arab empire expanded to the north, many

Jews, particularly those from the lower classes, immigrated to the frontiers. Settled far from the central authorities, they objected to the high taxes and religious dogma imposed by the *gaon*. Their Arab neighbors on the frontiers rebelled against their own authorities and founded movements like Shiism to demand political and economic change.

Historians believe the Jewish dissenters were the original Karaites. They were drawn together by their rejection of the rabbis and the Talmud as well as their desire for equality and freedom. They insisted that the Bible is the only authoritative guide to Jewish law and that each Jew has the right and obligation to interpret it on his own. Karaites also passionately yearned for the return to Zion and the restoration of the Temple in Jerusalem.

The leader to commit Karaite beliefs to writing was Anan ben David, a member of an aristocratic Rabbanite family who was born in the middle of the eighth century C.E. His *Book of Precepts* is the oldest existing Karaite document. The book developed a prayer service modeled on the services at the ancient Temple. Anan proposed two daily prayers, at dawn and sunset, just as there had been two daily sacrifices at the Temple. (The Rabbanites had added a third service in the afternoon.) He agreed with the Rabbanites that sacrifices should not be performed until the Temple was rebuilt. Like the Rabbanites, he proposed that readings from the Bible would substitute for sacrifices by the priests.

Anan departed from the Rabbanites, however, by proposing that the readings in the synagogue should be limited to passages from the Five Books of Moses and the Book of Psalms and that only descendants of priests could read from them. He also differed by writing that the synagogue, like the Temple, should be uncontaminated and pure. Worshipers should wash their feet and hands before entering, he wrote. Anan's most radical departure was his view that worshipers should kneel before the ark, just as their ancestors had kneeled before the original ark of the covenant in the Temple. Anan's work was widely criticized by others who had split from the Rabbanites. Yet he later became known as the father of Karaism, and his teachings had a strong influence on the emerging sect.

Rabbanites maintained friendly relations with the dissidents for several generations after Anan, confident that their small following posed little danger to rabbinic Judaism. The good will ended when the Ananites and other similar sects were confronted by a polemical attack from a famous Rabbanite scholar, Saadiah al-Fayyumi, a tenth-century *gaon* from one of the rabbinic academies. Saadiah viewed the rebels as apostates and demanded they be ostracized. His attacks began a rift between Karaites and Rabbanites that would last for centuries. They also helped Karaism become a more organized movement.

In the middle of the tenth century, the center of Karaism shifted from Persia to Syria, ancient Israel, and Egypt, as the dissidents became missionaries and spread their teachings. The Karaite Academy in Jerusalem produced scholars who crafted great literary works. Their followers lived in self-imposed poverty, mourned for the return of the Temple, and fasted at least twice a week.

At one time, there were as many Karaites as Rabbanites in Jerusalem. Most of the Jerusalem Jewish community was wiped

out during the Crusades that began at the close of the eleventh
century. Survivors of the Karaite community resettled in
Ashkelon as well as in Cairo and Damascus.

THE KARAITE MOVEMENT achieved perhaps its
greatest prominence in Egypt toward the end of the nineteenth
century under British rule. By the time Eliyahu and Nehama
were born, there were about 7,000 Karaites in Cairo. They had
two synagogues and two Karaite schools, one for girls and one
for boys.

The Karaite quarter covered about half a square mile.
Karaites thrived as engineers, doctors, and lawyers; the community also produced several important artists, poets, and com-
posers. The wealthier Karaite families worked in banking, made
jewelry, and owned record companies and food-processing plants.
Some of them, like Eliyahu's family, eventually moved to more
fashionable neighborhoods in Cairo and its suburbs.

The Egyptian Karaites adopted many Arab customs and practices. Unlike Rabbanite Jews, they blended in with the natives
and dressed and spoke like their Muslim neighbors. Arabic was
the language of instruction in Karaite schools, and Karaites even
used Arabic terms, not Hebrew ones, to identify contested territories in Israel, such as Jerusalem. Karaite men wore baggy
pants and fezzes like Egyptian men, and most Karaite women
wore the Arab *chador*, although some of the wealthier and more
educated Karaites, like upper-class Egyptians, dressed in Western clothing. It was considered a compliment when a Muslim
told a Karaite, "Too bad you are a Jew."

Nonetheless, the Karaites developed close social and cultural ties with Rabbanites. They lived nearby—the Karaite quarter was adjacent to the Rabbanite quarter—and Karaites and Rabbanites often worked together in the same businesses.

Eliyahu, like many Karaite boys, joined the Young Karaite Jewish Association, which encouraged Karaites to establish a modern identity and reject isolation from the Rabbanite and Egyptian communities. The association published a bimonthly newsletter in Arabic, formed a Karaite boy scout troop, and sponsored an orchestra, theater group, sports activities, and field trips to the pyramids and other sites. Eliyahu also served as secretary of the Karaite religious council and rabbinic court.

Eliyahu was fifteen and Nehama was five when, in May 1948, Israel declared statehood and five Arab nations invaded. The Karaites had prayed fervently for the return to Zion, yet it had been a spiritual and abstract belief, not a political one. The existence of the State of Israel obliterated that distinction and made life increasingly difficult for them.

The Israeli defeat of the Arabs unleashed anger toward the Egyptian Jews, both Karaites and Rabbanites. Members of the Society of Muslim Brothers, a radical Islamic group, spoke openly about ridding Egypt of its Jews and sponsored public demonstrations and rallies to stir up anti-Jewish sentiment. On June 20, 1948, a bomb explosion in the Karaite quarter killed twenty-two people and wounded forty-one. Over the next three months, explosions destroyed Jewish-owned department stores, movie theaters, and other businesses in Cairo and killed dozens. On September 22, an explosion in the Rabbanite quarter killed nineteen people and wounded sixty-two. Several Cairo newspapers suggested that the explosions were a result of the animosity between Karaites and Rabbanites or came from bombs dropped by phantom Israeli airplanes. Most members of the Jewish community blamed the attacks on the Muslim Brothers. There was another possible source for the bombing that drew little attention. Terrorist attacks in the Baghdad Jewish community in 1951, including a hand grenade thrown into a crowded synagogue courtyard, were later linked to the Israeli underground as part of an effort to stimulate Jewish emigration to Israel.

Nearly one-third of Egypt's Jews left the country between 1948 and 1951, most of them for Israel. Only a handful of the emigrants were Karaites. Among them was Nehama's family—her parents, her four sisters, and a brother—who sailed to France and then entered Israel early in 1949. After some debate, the State of Israel had agreed to accept the Karaites under the Law of Return. Some rabbinic officials fought the decision. "Heaven forfend that we should bring this deadly plague into Israel's vineyard," the chief Ashkenazic rabbi of Jerusalem said at the time. The Interior Ministry labeled each immigrant as a "Karaite" or "Karaite Jew" on their identity cards; they were classified as members of a non-Jewish minority, like Christians and Muslims, in the 1952 census.

Nehama's family first lived with her uncle in a small aluminum hut in Ramla, eight of them sharing two beds. They later moved into an abandoned building nearby, which they occupied for several months. In 1951, they moved to Moshav Ranen, an agricultural settlement for North African immigrants, where they raised livestock and Nehama attended school.

Most Karaites in Egypt held on to the hope that they could remain part of Egyptian society even as Jews were asked to resign or retire from government positions and the Muslim Brothers attacked Jewish and foreign businesses and looted and burned a Rabbanite school. Their continued optimism was reflected in a May 1951 Karaite community newspaper, which dedicated most of one issue to celebrating King Faruq's second marriage. Karaite poets composed verses for the occasion.

Eliyahu's family had few thoughts about emigrating, even after Eliyahu was forced to leave school. Just before the war with Israel began in 1948, Eliyahu had applied to attend a government school that trained accountants. He never received a response. That fall, he returned to his high school. He attended an assembly on the first day, where class assignments were announced. Eliyahu waited patiently but his name was never called. As the assembly broke up, he talked with a Christian student he had just met, who said he was worried about Eliyahu's safety. Perhaps, he advised Eliyahu, it would be better if he didn't return to school.

With few options for work or schooling, Eliyahu volunteered to work at a factory that manufactured jewelry, owned by a wealthy Karaite. Because of Eliyahu's interest in accounting, the owner of the factory trained Eliyahu to do the books. Within a few months, he was handling all of the factory's accounting work.

The political conditions for Egypt's Jews continued to deteriorate. In July 1952, a military coup overthrew the monarchy with the support of the Muslim Brothers. The new government maintained friendly relations with the Jewish community until

Gamel Abdel Nasser, one of the officers, became head of state in 1954. That year, Egyptian authorities arrested a Karaite physician, Dr. Moshe Marzouk, and twelve other Jews and charged them with conducting espionage and committing sab- otage for Israeli army intelligence. They were tried and con- victed; Marzouk was hanged in January 1955.

Israel launched an attack on Gaza in February, apparently in retaliation for Dr. Marzouk's execution. The Suez/Sinai War followed in the fall of 1956, with Israeli forces temporarily seiz- ing the Sinai peninsula and British and French forces invading Egypt to protect the Suez Canal. In the succeeding months, the Egyptian government expelled thousands of British and French citizens, detained about 1,000 Jews, and closed down hun- dreds of Jewish businesses. Nasser proclaimed that Zionists could not hold Egyptian citizenship.

Karaites like the Dabbachs, who had remained loyal Egyp- tians despite the increasing animosity toward Jews, no longer felt safe. The Dabbachs' Algerian citizenship, which they had purchased at the consulate in Cairo before Eliyahu was born, had helped protect them in the past. Now it branded them as allies of the hated French. (Nearly half of Egypt's Jews held for- eign citizenship so they could serve as local representatives for foreign businesses. Most of the other Jews were stateless; there had long been a maze of bureaucratic barriers to discourage non- Muslims from applying for Egyptian citizenship.)

At the end of 1956, a military officer visited the Dabbachs and ordered them to leave Egypt within a week. He said that as allies of the French they no longer were welcome. The fam- ily quickly arranged a wedding for Eliyahu's younger brother,

Moshe, who had planned to be married a few months later. The Dabbachs then sailed via Europe for Israel, arriving early in 1957. Most of the remaining Egyptian Jews emigrated in the following months.

The Dabbachs lived in Ofakim, where they worked in building construction. Eliyahu was drafted into the Israeli army. He served for thirty months, the required enlistment period at the time. After he completed his army service, Eliyahu lived in an unfinished house one of his uncles was building in Moshav Ranen. His uncle, convinced it was time for Eliyahu to marry, introduced him to Nehama. Her parents were worried about her marriage prospects, since she was already seventeen; Karaite girls were customarily married by age fifteen, although Israeli law prohibited marriage before age seventeen. Eliyahu re-enlisted in the army, and Nehama worked as a seamstress for a year so they could raise money for their wedding.

By the time Nehama and Eliyahu were married, there were more than 7,000 Karaites in Israel, nearly all of them from Egypt. Most of them lived at first in agricultural settlements and then moved to the cities, particularly Ashdod and Ramla, where many Karaites worked as jewelers and goldsmiths. Eliyahu and Nehama moved to Ashdod, near the base where Eliyahu worked. Their only child, a daughter, was born in 1968. They named her Latifa, after the aunt who had raised Eliyahu.

The eye problems that had plagued his aunt and other members of his family affected Eliyahu as well. He retired from the army when he was forty-six and legally blind. Nehama supported them by working as a nurse for the elderly. Eliyahu volunteered as a health-care worker, and his friends eventually helped him establish a community center for the blind in Ramla. Eliyahu also worked as a volunteer religious leader for the Karaite community.

THE EGYPTIAN KARAITES built a synagogue in Ramla in 1961 and opened one in Ashdod in 1982. They also established a headquarters, which they call the Karaite World Center, in Ramla. As in Egypt, the community is led by a national council, composed of delegates from Karaite settlements throughout Israel. A religious council of Karaite rabbis, called *hachamim,* decides questions of religious law. There are no Karaite schools; the community established a *yeshiva* several years ago to train rabbis but closed it due to a shortage of funds.

Although the Orthodox Jews who control religious affairs in Israel have officially recognized Karaites as Jews, Karaite religious leaders have no legal standing. They are permitted to officiate at marriages and divorces only within their own community. There are only a handful of Karaite marriages. Karaites have a much more strict interpretation of the laws of incest than Rabbanite Jews, and prohibit marriage between even distant relatives. Since such a large number of Egyptian Karaites are related to one another, young people are unlikely to find marriage partners within the community. In most cases, they marry Rabbanite Jews they meet in school or in the army. Under Israeli law, Karaites who wish to marry Rabbanite Jews are required to study with an Orthodox rabbi for several days and undergo a ceremony witnessed by three rabbis in which they promise to abandon Karaite customs. The net effect of their recognition by Israeli religious authorities has been the gradual dissolution and assimilation of the Egyptian Karaite community in Israel.

Most of the Karaite rabbis, like Eliyahu, are now in their sixties and seventies; there are no young rabbis in training. Community leaders complain that the ultra-Orthodox Jews who control religious affairs in Israel are providing the Karaites with only half of the funding given to other religious communities of their size. "We are being discriminated against and deprived of our rights," *Hacham* Chaim Levy, an intense, white-haired man who was formerly head of the Karaite religious community, tells me. "Our budget from the state is so small that ninety percent of our staff gets no salary. Even the slaves were paid in biblical times."

Levy and other religious Karaites have retained many of their ancient customs and beliefs. Religious Karaites still worship twice a day and wear prayer shawls with one blue string. They do not wear *tefillin*, as Orthodox Jewish men do, placing passages from the Torah near their hearts and on their foreheads based on biblical instructions to keep God's words "upon your heart . . . [and to] tie them for a sign upon your hand and for a remembrance between your eyes." Karaites believe the passage is simply a figure of speech reminding Jews to remember the Torah.

Karaite beliefs are based on what they call the "plain meaning" of the Bible. Before Passover, for example, Karaites use up all of their *hametz*, or leavened foods. The Karaites consider the practice of temporarily selling or giving away *hametz*, followed by most Rabbanites, to be a sham. Unlike religious Rabbanites, Karaites will eat milk with meat, taking only literally the biblical commandment that prohibits eating the meat of a kid with its mother's milk. Unlike Rabbanite Jews, who encourage sex on the Sabbath as a way to celebrate it, Karaites prohibit sexual intercourse on the Sabbath.

Religious Karaites also follow stricter laws of ritual purity than Rabbanites. During menstruation and after the birth of a child, Karaite women are segregated in a corner of the house and have no contact with others. Karaite laws on divorce and paternity are more liberal. Karaite women have an equal right to seek a divorce, unlike Orthodox Jews. Karaites believe men, not women, pass on their religious identity to their children.

Ancient Karaites observed Jewish holidays on different dates than Rabbanite Jews did, basing their calendars on observations of the moon and the ripening of the barley crop in Israel. Today there is wide disagreement among religious Karaites; there are as many as four different Karaite calendars. Most Karaites have adapted to Israeli culture and follow the Rabbanite calendar.

There are no reliable estimates of how many Karaites now live in Israel; Karaite custom prohibits an official census. Community leaders say privately that there are roughly 25,000 Karaites in Israel today; others say there are no more than 10,000 or 15,000. The number of religious Karaites is far smaller. Very few of the second and third generations of Egyptian Karaites who came to Israel attend synagogue services or follow Karaite practices at home. Like most Israelis, they have become secular and have left religion to the rabbis.

"Our young people are torn between two different worlds," Eliyahu tells me. "They are Israelis on the outside, but many live as Karaites inside their homes. I can only hope that my three grandchildren will keep our traditions."

In an effort to preserve their history, the Karaites have begun work on a museum in Jerusalem run by Eliyahu's brother, Moshe, who also is a rabbi. It is located in Old Jerusalem in a thirteenth-century stone building that contains the Anan Synagogue, named in honor of the founder of Karaism. Some modern-day Karaites believe it was built by Anan in the eighth century, although the architecture is clearly from the Crusader era. So far, the museum includes mannequins under a *chuppah* in wedding costumes, photographs of Egyptian *hachamim,* copies of marriage contracts, and books.

THE LURE OF secular culture and the Orthodox rabbinic dominance of religious life in Israel have taken their toll on the Egyptian Karaites. Yet even as their young people assimilate into modern Israeli life, Karaite leaders rarely accept converts and remain distant from outsiders. They are particularly distrustful of reporters; the occasional story about Karaites in the Israeli press most often compares them to Muslims, ridiculing them for removing their shoes and bowing during worship.

One hope for reviving Karaism in Israel rests with emigrants from the former Soviet Union who are discovering Karaite roots. In June 1998, under the sponsorship of the Liaison Bureau of the Israeli prime minister's office, Levy and another Karaite religious leader visited some of the Karaite communities in Poland and the Crimea. They estimated that there are thousands of Karaites there who hid their identity for generations. Many of them, Levy said, are now eager to settle in Israel.

Karaites first settled in the Crimea in the twelfth century and lived comfortably among the Tartars. They worked as farmers, growing tobacco and cucumbers and raising livestock, spoke the local Turkish dialect, and intermarried with their non-Jewish neighbors. Later generations of Karaites became shopkeepers and owned tanneries as the community grew in wealth and status. Karaites were exempted from paying taxes.

Karaite settlements farther to the west were founded late in the fourteenth century when the Duke of Lithuania defeated the Tartars and resettled several hundred Karaite families in Lithuanian cities, where they helped the kingdom expand foreign trade. In Troki, near Vilna, the Karaites were given their own courts and complete religious and commercial freedom. Karaites became officers in the army, served in local government, and were considered members of the lower aristocracy. They had friendly relations with their neighbors until the middle of the seventeenth century, when the Cossacks, led by Bogdan Chmielnicki, revolted against the nobles and, with the help of Russian peasants, massacred hundreds of thousands of Eastern European Jews, both Rabbanites and Karaites.

The massacres, European wars, and continuing persecutions of the seventeenth and eighteenth centuries led the remaining Karaites to further separate themselves from the Rabbanites. Some dressed and spoke like Poles and Lithuanians. Eventually they would claim they were not Jews.

Late in the eighteenth century, the Russian czars took control over Lithuania. In 1795, the Karaites successfully petitioned Catherine the Great to exempt them from the double tax imposed on Jews and to permit them to acquire land. Karaites later received an exemption from military service. They argued that they were different from the Rabbanites because they did not accept the Talmud and were more loyal, hardworking, and honest. Divisions between Karaites and Rabbanites widened; the Karaites even campaigned for the expulsion of the Rabbanites from Troki. Rabbanites were banned from the city for nearly thirty years.

In Russia, the Karaites thrived as wealthy landowners while the Rabbanites generally worked as peddlers and craftsmen. They spoke Russian or Ukrainian and produced music and literature in the local languages. Karaites used their status to gain official recognition as "Russian Karaites of the Old Testament Faith," rather than as Jews, and later were recognized simply as Karaites. The czars treated them as if they were an independent religion and in 1863 gave them the same rights as Christians. By 1897 they became the largest (about 13,000 people) and wealthiest Karaite center in the world.

One of the most prominent Karaites of the nineteenth century, Abraham Firkovich, collected ancient manuscripts from Israel and Egypt and published articles further distancing the Karaites from the Jews. He claimed the manuscripts proved that Karaites had a distinct identity and that they should not be held responsible for Christ's crucifixion because they had settled in the Crimea seven hundred years before Christ was born. He also claimed that Khazar nobles, who ruled an empire north of the Caspian Sea until the end of the tenth century, had converted to Karaism about the year 740 and that many of their subjects became Karaites. Most scholars had concluded that the Khazars were converts to Rabbanite Judaism.

There is little basis for Firkovich's thesis. He falsified dates to support his claims about the age of the Karaite community in the Crimea, and forged or altered many of his documents. Yet his arguments convinced the czars to grant full civil rights to the Karaites. His work later was used to help Karaites avoid Nazi persecution.

After the Bolshevik Revolution, the Communists resettled all the Karaites in the Crimea, and many of them suffered under the Soviet collectivization of agriculture. The Nazis, who courted support from the Tartar, Turkish, and Caucasian minorities in the Soviet Union, found some ardent collaborators and allies among the Karaites. In 1938, a group of Karaites living in Germany petitioned the Reich to consider them Karaites, not Jews. After the German army drove the Russians out of eastern Poland and Lithuania, the *hacham* of the Polish Karaite community received a proclamation from the Nazis in 1941 that his followers were not Jewish. The Nazis issued a similar exemption for the Crimean Karaites. After an investigation, the policy was confirmed by an official communiqué in June 1943 recognizing the Karaites as a separate ethnic minority. The Karaites, like the Georgian and Mountain Jews, were saved from the Holocaust.

Some Karaites worked for the Nazis as interpreters. A survivor of the Lutsk ghetto accused Karaites of extorting money from leaders of the Jewish community, beating up women and children, and helping the Nazis liquidate the ghetto in August

1942. By late 1944, 500 to 600 Karaites—apparently police and auxiliary army officers from the Crimea who had retreated to the west—were serving in the Waffen SS and the Tartar division of the German army. But only a few hundred Karaites carried out atrocities; others used their special status to assist Rabbanite Jews. With the Karaites' help, some Rabbanites escaped persecution and extermination by forging documents falsely identifying them as Karaites.

In the postwar years, most of the Crimean and European Karaites assimilated into their surrounding communities and abandoned their religious practices. Many of them, however, retained some customs, such as eating special foods for holidays, and tended to marry within the Karaite community.

A few of the Russian Karaites who have come to Israel in recent years have sought to affiliate themselves with the Egyptian Karaite community. But the historical and traditional differences between the two communities seem to rule out any significant revival of Karaism in Israel among Russian immigrants. There may be one other hope for the future of the Karaites. It comes from outside the community.

NEHEMIA GORDON WAS eleven years old when he first decided he wanted to be a Karaite. It was 1983 and he was a student at a Jewish day school in Chicago. His class had been studying Talmud, the oral law, for several years, but Nehemia was troubled by it. A number of passages in the Bible said the Torah was the word of God, perfect and complete, and nothing should be added to it or subtracted from it. Why, then, Nehemia asked himself, was there another set of laws based on an oral tradition?

He brought his questions to the rabbis at his day school. They told him that both the Torah and the oral law came from God and both were correct. Nehemia wasn't convinced. The more he studied, the more he doubted the Talmud. His beliefs were reinforced when he read about King Josiah. In the seventh century B.C.E., Josiah ordered repairs to the Temple in Jerusalem. During the renovations, according to the Second Book of Kings, the high priest discovered the long-lost book of laws God had given to Moses. Jews from around the kingdom came to Jerusalem to hear the words read. Based on the text, Josiah banned idol-worshiping cults, purged the Temple of idols, and commanded his people to again follow Mosaic law. For the first time, Jews in Jerusalem celebrated Passover as commanded in the Torah. To Nehemia, the story implied that the oral law was the work of man, not God. If the Jews had lost the written Torah in Josiah's time, Nehemia reasoned, and didn't know that it was wrong to worship idols, it seemed impossible that they could have preserved an oral law handed down since Moses. He felt as if he were like King Josiah, rediscovering the true Torah.

Nehemia shared his opinions with his classmates, who argued with him and made fun of him, calling him a Karaite. Nehemia had heard the term before but had only a vague idea of what it meant. He looked it up in an old *World Book Encyclopedia*, which identified Karaism as a sect of Judaism that refused to accept oral law. The encyclopedia said that only a few hundred Karaites remained, mostly in Egypt.

Nehemia was encouraged. He wasn't the only one who held these beliefs. He dreamed of traveling to Egypt—he thought of it as a land of crocodiles—and searching for Karaites. Nehemia began to follow Karaite practices at home, based on his reading of the Bible. He refused to eat hot food on the Sabbath, the *cholent* that his mother had left in a warm oven. His mother eventually agreed to serve him cold food. He attended services in his synagogue only occasionally; many of the Rabbanite prayers and practices seemed to have no basis in the Torah. Nehemia's father, who had been ordained as a rabbi but was a practicing attorney, at first tried to convince him he was wrong. He eventually dismissed Nehemia's actions as part of a phase that would go away, like other youthful fascinations.

It didn't. When Nehemia was in the tenth grade, a family friend told him she actually knew a Karaite who had been her classmate at the local Jewish high school. Nehemia was thrilled; he had been unsure if there were any Karaites left outside of a handful in Egypt. He couldn't find the man's name in the Chicago telephone book, but he did find his picture—and the correct spelling of his name—in a school yearbook. Nehemia was disappointed when he called him on the telephone. The man told Nehemia that he was related to Karaites yet knew nothing about their history or practices. He referred him instead to an uncle who had been raised in Egypt and lived in Skokie, Illinois.

The uncle told Nehemia a little about the history of the Egyptian Karaites. He said he hadn't continued to practice Karaism but he knew of a Karaite synagogue in California. Its founder and leader, Joe Pessah, was born in Cairo in 1945 and raised in a religious Karaite family. Among the last Jews to leave Egypt, Pessah had been arrested and imprisoned by Egyptian authorities after the Arab-Israeli war in 1967 and immigrated with his wife to the United States when he was released in 1970. There was a small Karaite community in California, the uncle said, that celebrated Rosh Hashanah and Yom Kippur together and met for social occasions. Pessah had helped organize the community and served as acting rabbi for the congregation.

"I tracked down Pessah's phone number and memorized it," Nehemia tells me more than a dozen years later. "I still know it today." Nehemia, now a student of biblical studies at Hebrew University in Jerusalem, is a heavyset young man with short brown hair who dresses casually, like most college students. Unlike other religious Jews, he doesn't wear a skullcap or fringes from a prayer shawl under his shirt.

"Until I talked to Pessah," Nehemia tells me as he sips a bottle of water in my hotel lobby, "I had thought I was the only one in the world who had these beliefs. He was very helpful and encouraging. From then on, I talked to him on the telephone every week. And I made plans to visit him and his congregation."

During winter vacation in 1988, when he was sixteen, Nehemia told his parents he was going to take a bus to California to visit a friend he had met the previous summer. But instead he visited Pessah and the Karaites. The fifty-hour journey to San Francisco proved to be an unusual experience for a sheltered teenager from a religious home who had never crossed the Mississippi.

"It was a weird trip," Nehemia recalls. "There was a bunch of Deadheads on the bus going to a Grateful Dead concert in San Francisco. The bus smelled of pot the whole way. I couldn't sleep on the bus, and I was exhausted and bored. We stopped at midnight in Salt Lake City and saw fog over the Mormon Temple. Then we stopped in Carson City and I played the slot machines."

Nehemia stayed with Pessah for a week and attended services in a room the Karaites rented from a Reform synagogue in Daly City. The congregation had revived Karaite rituals, specifically those of Egyptian Karaism.

"I think what Pessah has done is miraculous," Nehemia says, "because there was nothing before he arrived. The service seemed very biblical. We took off our shoes before we entered the room, and we bowed down when we prayed. It was a little awkward at first. After one of the breaks, I accidentally walked into the synagogue with my shoes on. But everyone was really kind to me and later talked with me for hours about Karaism. They said I was really welcome there."

Nehemia was disheartened, however, by the secularism of the California community. Few of them kept the Sabbath or observed even the most basic laws of Judaism. It seemed to him as if secularism was ingrained among Egyptian Karaites.

Nehemia learned that many of the remaining Egyptian Karaites had resettled in Israel. He hoped to visit them, although Pessah and the other congregants in California told him he probably wouldn't be welcomed there.

After he returned to Chicago, Nehemia continued to talk with Pessah by telephone. He tracked down some descendants of Karaites in Chicago and organized a Karaite prayer service for the High Holidays.

In his senior year of high school, Nehemia visited concentration camps in Poland and holy sites in Israel as part of a program called the March of the Living. In Jerusalem, he found a tourist map that showed the site of the Anan Synagogue. He broke away from the group to visit it; once inside, Nehemia gazed at the ancient walls, the Persian carpet, and the hanging ornaments, feeling a connection to the early days of Karaism. He returned later that week to attend Sabbath services and was impressed by the congregation's devotion to Karaite ritual. The following Tuesday, he participated in a study group at the synagogue led by Chaim Levy.

"They had this very learned discussion of whether one could eat cheese on Passover," Nehemia says. "These were people who really knew the Torah and read it on a very high level. I was encouraged by the fact that there were highly educated Karaites trying to follow the Bible."

When he completed high school in the summer of 1990, Nehemia went to California to serve as a counselor in a summer camp for young Karaites from around the United States. He returned to Israel the following year to work on a *kibbutz* and to study modern Hebrew. He visited his mother, who by then had moved to Israel and lived in Jerusalem, and attended more services and study groups at the Anan Synagogue. He met two other people, a young man from England and an older man from the United States, who also had adopted Karaism. The American, Mordecai Alfandari, descended from Egyptian Rabbanite Jews and had been living in Israel since the 1950s. He had become a practicing Karaite in Israel ("It was like becoming a Communist during the McCarthy era," Alfandari says). For several years, Alfandari published his own Karaite magazine, although the Karaite community didn't accept him. It wasn't until several years after Nehemia met him that the Egyptian Karaites officially recognized Alfandari as a Karaite. He had been a practicing Karaite for nearly forty years.

"Meeting these other people made me reassess things," Nehemia recalls. "I wasn't the only outsider who had adopted Karaism. Here were two other rational people from different backgrounds who had come to the same conclusion I had. They told me that the Egyptian Karaites could be very friendly on a personal level but would never accept an outsider on a religious level."

In 1991, Nehemia enrolled at Loyola University in Chicago and attended classes for a year. He and his girlfriend from high school, Devorah Bromberg, became engaged the following year and made plans for their wedding. Nehemia went to Israel in the spring to ask Levy if he would officiate at their wedding. Levy was planning an extended visit to Karaite communities in the United States and agreed to perform the wedding that August in Chicago. Nehemia's mother came from Israel, and Devorah's family from Chicago attended, along with members of the Karaite communities of Chicago and San Francisco. Nehemia's father didn't come. As an ordained Orthodox rabbi, he felt it would be sacrilegious to attend a Karaite wedding, even for his own son.

The wedding was a traditional Karaite ceremony, with

prayers sung responsively and Karaite poems recited, followed by the usual dancing, singing, and picture-taking. A few days after the wedding, in September 1993, Nehemia and Devorah resettled in Jerusalem. Nehemia now studies at Hebrew University, and Devorah works for a nongovernmental organization. They follow Karaite practices at home, and if they have children, they plan to raise them as Karaites.

Like Alfandari, his role model, Nehemia launched a Karaite publication. This one is on the World Wide Web and is called "The Karaite Korner." It includes pages on the history of the Karaites and explanations of Karaite laws, biblical exegesis, and the calendar. Unlike most modern-day Karaites, Nehemia follows the ancient method of determining the holidays. He celebrates Jewish holidays as much as a month later than other Jews do.

"Since we've been living here, my relations with the religious Karaites have improved," Nehemia says. "Some view me as a full-fledged Karaite, although there are still some who see me as a Rabbanite who practices Karaism.

"But there are very few religious Karaites left. Most of them want to be like everyone else—they want to be like the secular majority in Israel. Some families don't even tell their children they are Karaites."

Their name apparently derives from . . .   Nathan Schur, *The Karaite Encyclopedia* (New York: Verlag Peter Lang GmbH, 1995), pp. 213–14.

At one time, Karaism was a major branch . . .   Nathan Schur, *History of the Karaites* (New York: Verlag Peter Lang GmbH, 1992), pp. 156–60.

Tobiah Levi Babovitch, the *hacham* . . .   Schur, *The Karaite Encyclopedia*, p. 39.

Although some leaders of the Karaite community supported inter-marriage . . .   Joel Beinin, *The Dispersion of Egyptian Jewry* (Los Angeles: University of California Press, 1998), p. 3.

Most historians conclude that Karaism first emerged . . . the center of Karaism shifted from Persia . . .   Leon Nemoy, *Karaite Anthology: Excerpts from the Early Literature* (New Haven: Yale University Press, 1952), pp. xiii–xxvi.

At one time, there were as many Karaites . . .   Schur, *History of the Karaites,* p. 31.

The Karaite movement achieved perhaps its greatest prominence . . . Ibid., pp. 131–34.

Unlike Rabbanite Jews, they blended in with the natives . . . a spiritual and abstract belief . . .   Beinin, *The Dispersion of Egyptian Jewry,* pp. 39–43.

On June 20, 1948, a bomb explosion . . . blamed the attacks on the Muslim Brothers.   Ibid., pp. 68–70.

Nearly one-third of Egypt's Jews left . . .   Ibid., p. 70.

Some rabbinic officials fought the decision . . .   Tom Segev, *1949: The First Israelis* (New York: Free Press, 1986), p. 144.

Most Karaites in Egypt held on to the hope . . . composed verses for the occasion.   Beinin, *The Dispersion of Egyptian Jewry,* p. 72.

The political conditions for Egypt's Jews . . . Nasser proclaimed that Zionists could not hold Egyptian citizenship.   Ibid., pp. 85–87.

Nearly half of Egypt's Jews held foreign citizenship . . .   Ibid., pp. 37–38.

The Egyptian Karaites built a synagogue in Ramla . . . due to a shortage of funds.   Ibid., p. 182.

Karaite beliefs are based on . . . and the ripening of the barley crop in Israel.   Schur, *The Karaite Encyclopedia,* p. 15.

Karaites first settled in the Crimea . . . were saved from the Holocaust. Schur, *History of the Karaites,* pp. 102–25.

Some Karaites worked for the Nazis as interpreters. . . . by forging documents falsely identifying them as Karaites.   Schur, *History of the Karaites*, pp. 123–25; Simon Wiesenthal Center <http://motlc.wiesenthal.org/text/x12/xm1224.html>.

Its founder and leader, Joe Pessah . . .   Beinin, *The Dispersion of Egyptian Jewry*, pp. 190–91.

. . . Nehemia launched a Karaite publication.   <http://www.karaitekorner.org>.

EPILOGUE

Much has changed in these communities since I visited them. Since my March 1998 visit to Uganda, the Abayudaya have realized Kakungulu's dream of establishing their own school. They have enrolled more than 600 students in a primary school and are completing a new brick schoolhouse on Nabugoye Hill with government support. More than seventy students have enrolled in a new high school, headed by Gershom Sizomu, called Semei Kakungulu High School. The government has required the Abayudaya to build additional classrooms, a library, and staff houses before it can be accredited. Once electrical service is extended to Nabugoye, Gershom hopes to equip the school with computers and laboratory equipment and to offer classes in science and technical training. He also plans to teach classes on Hebrew and Jewish religion and culture.

The Abayudaya have completed the small guest house near the bottom of Nabugoye Hill but have not yet furnished it or equipped it with electricity or running water. It will have three bedrooms, a bathroom, and a sitting room. The community continues to raise funds for the schools and guest house by selling handmade skullcaps and a music album through its Web site. Community members are growing cotton so they can manufacture and sell their own prayer shawls.

Joab Keki has resigned as chairman of the Abayudaya community, and Aaron Kintu Moses has announced plans to succeed him. Aaron recently enrolled in Makerere University in Kampala. The Abayudaya Women's Association, headed by Aaron's wife, Naome, has received a donation of a dozen heifers from the Heifer Project.

The high death rate from disease and malnutrition among young men has exacerbated the shortage of unmarried males and threatens the future of the community. There have been very few marriages and births in recent years. An increasing number of young women are marrying outside the community.

SEGUNDO VILLANUEVA AND his brother, Álvaro, now live in Kfar Tapuach, a new West Bank settlement north of Eilon Moreh. The surrounding hills are dotted with Palestinian towns and villages. The entrance is guarded by Israeli soldiers with machine guns propped up on sandbags. There are about 100 small homes, all made of concrete, along one main road. The residents are recent immigrants, most of them Russians. The Villanueva house, painted red, is next door to the Peréz house, home of the only other Peruvian family in the village. It sits just a few yards from a tall razor-wire fence and a guard tower. Floodlights shine on the hard gray soil outside the fence.

The Villanuevas have no telephone; they come out to their neighbors' patio to talk while the Peréz children, with brown skin and black hair, jump off a picnic table, swing from a large hanging punching bag, and chase after chickens. The boys all have *peiot*, the sidecurls worn by ultra-Orthodox Jews.

Álvaro Villanueva, who wears a pistol on his right hip, is eager to talk, in both Hebrew and Spanish, about the congregation that he and his brother founded, helped train in Judaism, and brought to villages in the West Bank and Gaza Strip. Segundo, who is now called Tzidkiyahu, remains silent, almost sullen, staring out beyond the fence in the twilight. He looks to me like a prophet whose followers have abandoned him. He becomes animated only when the discussion turns to the peace agreements that may return Kfar Tapuach and other West Bank towns to the Palestinians. He angrily defends the settlers' rights to keep their homes.

While Segundo's son, Joshua, who is in his late thirties, lives in Jerusalem and is studying to be a rabbi, is aware of his history, the Peréz children know little about the story of how they came here. Many remaining members of the Villanuevas' congregations in Trujillo and Lima, which I visited in August 1998, still hope to undergo conversion and resettle in Israel.

SEVENTY MILES SOUTHWEST of Kfar Tapuach, in the Israeli-occupied Gaza Strip between Israel and Egypt, Joshua Benjamin, an Indian Jew whose grandfather and father inspired the Mizos to become Jews and settle in Israel, lives with his wife and four children. Their town, near Gush Katif, is called Newe Dekalim. It is a desert town with palm trees and hot, dry air, surrounded by squalid Palestinian camps and closely guarded by army police. The Benjamins' large house has a red-tiled roof. Most of their neighbors also are Indian immigrants, the B'nai Manasseh from Mizoram and Manipur.

Joshua's first job was as a dishwasher in a girls' school in Gush Katif. Then he worked in a printing firm, feeding machines with paper and cleaning them.

"My job in India as a draftsman was very easy and respectable and meaningful," Joshua says as his children race around their living room. "Here we are paid little, but my wife also works and we can afford to buy a house and luxuries like an air conditioner and a computer. I could never have these things in India.

"But I have no status here. I was respected and accepted in India. Here I am a nobody, just a guy in the streets. In Mizoram, when we have guests join the community from far away, we welcome them, we give all our attention to them. It's not that way in Israel. Maybe I was expecting too much."

Nonetheless, Joshua says it is a great *mitzvah* to live in Israel and to raise his children there. "Life is a bit difficult here.

Maybe after ten years I won't feel like a stranger. But I feel very good that my children are growing up in such a holy place."

Another nineteen members of B'nai Manasseh arrived in Israel later in the year, and dozens more are making plans to immigrate. Back in Mizoram, where I visited in March and April 1999, the community has been able to retain its synagogue in Aizawl. An elder in the Presbyterian church—Hmingrthanga (he has only one name, like most Mizos)—bought the building on behalf of the Jewish community; he told them they may pay him back whenever they can raise the funds.

WHEN I VISITED Rabbi Eliyahu Avichail in Jerusalem in August 1999, he told me that the Barak government had agreed to accept 100 new B'nai Manasseh each year. They will enter as temporary citizens, not tourists. But the government will not yet pay for their transportation and housing. Avichail is raising funds by giving lectures and by soliciting contributions from American donors. Some of the B'nai Manasseh who have settled in Israel also are contributing funds.

Avichail says he has no interest in bringing any more Peruvians to Israel, despite continuing appeals from those who remain in Trujillo and Lima.

"The first group that came, Villanueva's group, is a symbol of the best absorption in Israel," Avichail says. "In my opinion, there were too many in the second group. Some of the teenagers who came with their families were not motivated to be Jews and made some trouble after they came to Israel. It was time to stop the process. I was afraid we would have all of Peru wanting to come."

I then ask him what might happen if settlements in the West Bank and Gaza are turned over to the Palestinians. Avichail stiffens.

"The whole world will turn against Israel and they will try to take Jerusalem from us," he says angrily. "Then the son of Joseph will come to defeat Gog and Magog, the forces of evil, followed by the son of David, who will bring peace."

AFTER MY VISIT to the Amazon in January 1998, I kept in touch with the Benchayas by telephone and e-mail. Margarida now says she is considering converting to Judaism, despite her husband's continuing indifference to religious practice.

"I already consider myself Jewish," says Margarida, who grew up in a nonobservant Catholic family. "But I believe I have to study more to decide if I should convert. I need to see if I will be able to accomplish everything that this religion hopes to have from me."

As for Jaime, who recently shifted his political affiliation to the Liberal Social Party, Margarida says she and her daughters still hope he will formally return to the community and follow practices his ancestors abandoned when they came to the Amazon from Morocco.

"My daughters and I feel the need for the head of the family to participate in this," Margarida says. "We feel ahead of him in this aspect of life."

SINCE MY VISIT to Recife in December 1997 and January 1998, the Ashkenazic community has closed its synagogue on Martins Junior Street and is now restoring the historic Dutch synagogue from the 1640s, Tsur Israel. They plan to use it as a museum and cultural center documenting the history of Jewish life in Brazil.

Odmar wrote me that he no longer serves as president of the B'nai Anusim; he stepped down in a dispute with Ya'acov de Oliveira, the representative sent by Rabbi Sebag from Israel to work with the community. Oliveira spent only a month in Recife.

The congregation has split into two groups. One is led by Isaac Essoudry, and its members are worshiping with the Ashkenazic community and preparing for conversion. Several already have converted. The other group, led by Odmar, still considers the *anusim* to be Jews and refuses to accept conversion. A Moroccan rabbi from São Paulo is serving as their religious advisor, and they conduct services in their homes. Luciano Lopes, the brilliant young Marrano student, has left for Israel to study in a *yeshiva*.

MORDECAI ALFANDARI, WHO helped inspire Nehemia Gordon to become a Karaite, died early in September 1999, shortly after I met him in Israel. He had seemed reluctant to talk with me and avoided any criticism of the Karaite community that once had shunned him. Nehemia says Mordecai knew he would die soon and feared the Karaites wouldn't bury him in their cemetery if he disparaged them. His fears, Nehemia wrote me, were unfounded.

Although the Karaite community had treated him as an outsider while he was alive, it honored Mordecai as a Karaite after he died, Nehemia wrote. He was buried in the Karaite cemetery in Jerusalem, and the community agreed to add the title *hacham* (wise man) to his tombstone. Thirty-five people, most of them Karaites, attended his funeral, and all of the Karaite synagogues in Israel read prayers in his memory.

AFTERWORD

At the end of my travels, I am left with many wonderful rec-
ollections: singing at two-year-old Daffna's birthday party
and visiting Eli Kagwa's half-finished synagogue in Uganda;
waking up to the sounds of prayer on a Sabbath morning in a
synagogue in Peru; celebrating Passover with flat *chapatis* and
unfamiliar bitter herbs in India; discovering Jewish gravestones
in the Amazon; joining in Torah study with Marranos in a
crumbling synagogue in Recife; and sharing a Sabbath lunch
with Egyptian Karaites in Israel.

The communities I visited are now part of my own life as a
Jew. My son, Marcus, wears a *kippah* from Peru when we light
candles on Friday nights. I often wear a *tallis* from India or a *kip-*

pah from Uganda to synagogue on Saturday mornings. When we share the Jewish holidays with friends and family members, we borrow customs, songs, and rituals from an ever-widening range of Jewish life. Like the communities I visited, we too are reshaping and reinventing Jewish life as we try to preserve Jewish tradition. Yet as my commitment to Judaism grows stronger, I am increasingly uncertain about which rituals, customs, and values are central to Jewish life.

The Karaites challenged rabbinic Judaism and the oral law yet remained Jews. Today, those who continue to practice as Karaites are a reminder that Islam and Judaism emerged from the same soil and that Judaism has abandoned many of its ancient practices, such as removing one's shoes in the synagogue and kneeling during prayer. They also raise questions about accepted Jewish practices. Is it the true meaning of the Hebrew Bible that Jews must separate all dairy products from all meat and must wear *tefillin*? Do Orthodox interpretations of Jewish law, such as permitting the use of automatic timers and special elevators on the Sabbath, violate the intent of some biblical commandments?

As the Karaites are vanishing, other communities are evolving, strengthening ancient ties, returning to lost traditions, or creating new ones. The Marranos who hope to return pose a powerful challenge to Judaism by their sheer numbers and growing popularity. Throughout the world, tens of thousands of people with Portuguese and Spanish ancestry are searching for Jewish roots. Some—like those in Recife and Belmonte, Portugal—are embracing Orthodox practices. Others are looking for more cultural connections. Particularly in Latin America,

those who see themselves as descendants of Marranos have discovered an affinity for the Jewish people. Some seek to convert
formally, in conventional and unconventional ways. The Web
site of the Templo Judaico Marranista, based in Rio de Janiero,
offers an online application and claims to provide an opportunity for people of any age, sexual preference, religion, race, or
color to become Jewish.

The descendants of Jews in the Amazon are returning to
their Sephardic Moroccan roots while at the same time incorporating Portuguese, African, and Christian beliefs and customs. As Jews have done for millennia, the young people in
Manaus are combining ancient traditions with the surrounding
culture and inventing a new form of Judaism that is both mystical and modern.

In northeastern India, the Mizos have linked their tribal traditions to biblical origins. Perhaps, as scholars believe happened
with the Ethiopian Jews, those connections were first suggested
by Christian missionaries and later became part of their legend.
If that is the case, the Mizos have closed a circle of Jewish history. As Christianity emerged from Judaism, Judaism is now
emerging from Christianity. But if the B'nai Manasseh are in fact
descendants of the Lost Tribes, they would force another rewrit-
ing of Jewish history.

The converts from Peru now living in Israel already have
made history. They emerged from a devotion to the text of the
Torah that echoed that of the Karaites, and participated in the
first Jewish mass conversion since the Idumeans and Galileans
more than 2,200 years ago. Their story is a reminder that in
the right political climate, Orthodox authorities are willing to

train and convert people who have no apparent Jewish ancestry. But the Orthodox conversions of both the Peruvians and Indians also raise some troubling questions. Are ultra-Orthodox Jews exploiting them to serve as human shields in the occupied territories? Or are they simply providing them with the life in Israel that they themselves desperately sought? And what will become of those who have been left behind in Peru and India? Will they develop new forms of Christian-Jewish practices?

The Abayudaya are perhaps unique. From their beginnings, they have been eager to learn about Judaism and adopt Orthodox practices. Yet Rabbi Avichail says he has no plans to help the Abayudaya come to Israel and has not replied to their letters. Avichail says the Abayudaya wouldn't fit in.

"They shouldn't come here because none of their boys could marry a Jewish girl," Avichail says.

When I ask if he thinks the Abayudaya could marry Ethiopian Jews, he indicates that he has no more to say on the subject. Ethiopian Jews now living in Israel have faced discrimination throughout the society, and their brethren in Ethiopia face continuing barriers to immigration from Israeli authorities. Is there no more room for black Africans in Israel?

There are dozens of other groups throughout the world that are creating new forms of Judaism. A group of Maoris in New Zealand has claimed descent from the Tribe of Judah. They customarily observe the Sabbath on Saturday and celebrate Passover on July 12, although many of their practices have moved closer to Christianity. In Turkey, some descendants of the Sabbateans, followers of a seventeenth-century mystic who declared himself the Messiah, now hope to be accepted as Jews once again. The Lemba in South Africa have been linked with ancient Jewish priests through DNA testing, although identifying Jews as a biological group seems ill-conceived, particulary after the Nazi's attempt to define and eliminate Jews as a race.

The most serious challenge to Orthodox authorities, however, comes from Reform, Conservative, and secular Jews in the United States and Israel. They have opened the doors of Judaism, ordaining women rabbis and welcoming intermarried couples, gays, and people from nearly every racial and ethnic group. Some Jews have embraced the study of Buddhism and other Eastern religions. As Orthodox leaders seem to become even more inflexible, American and Israeli Jews have fostered an explosion of new ideas and customs that cross all cultural barriers and make it virtually impossible to adhere to a narrow definition of who is a Jew. Is Judaism a religion, defined by belief in one God and observance of certain practices? Is it a people, restricted to those with Jewish ancestry? Or is Judaism primarily a culture and sense of community?

These uncertain boundaries raise other difficult questions. If there are no central authorities or clear criteria to determine who is a Jew, is there any practice, trait, gene, or custom that we can identify as unquestionably Jewish? Or are we faced with such broad diversity that Judaism is self-defined, that one can be Jewish simply by declaring oneself a Jew? We can find the answer, I believe, only if we are willing to challenge our biases and rethink our assumptions.

Acknowledgments

The people who made this book possible were my kind and generous hosts in the communities I visited: Gershom Sizomu; his wife, Zipporah; Aaron Kintu Moses and his wife, Naome, in Uganda; Rosa and Lucy Valderrama in Peru; Odmar Braga in Brazil; and Karaite spokesman Dvir Yosef in Israel.

I am particularly indebted to Itamar Guetta, an Israeli student from Ashdod. He took an immediate interest in my work when we met at the Valderramas' hostel in Trujillo, and he served as a translator when my Spanish failed me. He generously offered to let me stay with his family in Ashdod when I visited Israel, made arrangements for my visits with the Karaites, and served as driver, translator, and contributor to my understanding of Jewish law while we traveled to the West Bank, Gaza, Ramla, and Jerusalem.

In India, I am indebted to Mrs. Zaithanchhungi and her daughter Annette, Mizos who are practicing Christians closely affiliated with members of B'nai Manasseh. They fed and housed me, drove me throughout Aizawl, translated dozens of interviews, and tenaciously tracked down information for months after my visit. Their hospitality and kindness are unmatched.

My inspiration for this book came from Steve Sadow, a friend and colleague who is a professor of modern languages at Northeastern University in Boston. Steve introduced me to the rich culture and diversity of Jewish life in Latin America, where I first began to search for fragile branches. He helped me write, research, and conduct interviews for the chapter on the Peruvian Jews, including ones that required several long telephone conversations with Segundo Villanueva. Debra Kaufman, a sociology professor and chair of the Jewish Studies program at Northeastern, offered valuable insights that helped me frame the perspectives reflected in the Introduction and Afterword.

My dearest friend, Paul Wilkes, was, as always, a source of encouragement and support. He read early drafts of several chapters and helped me make them come to life. Laurel Leff, another colleague at Northeastern University, helped edit the Introduction and the first three chapters.

I also wish to thank Rabbi Jacques Cukierkorn, who offered advice and criticism and served as my guide and translator in Brazil and the Amazon. He supplied me with a variety of sources and was always available by e-mail for quick answers to questions about Jewish law or Brazilian food.

Karen Fischer, a graduate student in journalism at Northeastern, assisted me with invaluable research for nearly every chapter. She provided clear and thorough answers to a wide range of complicated historical questions. I could not have completed this book without her help. Ana Ilha, another Northeastern graduate student, helped by conducting and translating follow-up interviews with the Benchayas and Odmar Braga. Lee Malcus, a graduate student in anthropology at Boston University who has spent months living with the Abayudaya, offered much useful advice and editing on chapter 1. Jacob Meskin, a teacher and scholar of Jewish studies, advised me on questions of Jewish law and scholarship. The Provost's Office at Northeastern University provided me with a generous grant to help me complete my research and travels.

In addition, I wish to thank my agent, Gordon Kato, who believed in me and my idea and coached me as I developed it into a book proposal. My editor, Cindy Spiegel, read some early drafts and helped me find the right voice and tone; her thorough editing of my final draft added clarity and insight.

Finally, and most important, my love and gratitude go to my wife, Irene, and my son, Marcus. They endured my frequent trips abroad and the long hours when I was closeted in my study. As always, Irene was a patient listener and a kind and careful reader. And Marcus, who was born as I began my research, now has another book for his father to read to him, and, in perhaps not too many years, for him to read.